MW00650816

Advanced Portfolio Management

A Quant's Guide
for Fundamental Investors

Advanced Portfolio Management

A Quant's Guide
for Fundamental Investors

Giuseppe A. Paleologo

WILEY

Published by John Wiley & Sons, Inc., Hoboken, New Jersey.
Published simultaneously in Canada.

For general information on our other products and services please contact our Customer Care Department in the U.S. at 877-762-2974, outside the U.S. at 317-572-3993 or fax 317-572-4002.

Wiley also publishes its books in a variety of electronic formats. Some content that appears in print, however, may not be available in electronic format.

Library of Congress Cataloging-in-Publication Data is Available:

ISBN 9781119789796 (Hardback)
ISBN 9781119789819 (epdf)
ISBN 9781119789802 (epub)

Cover Design: Wiley
Cover Image: © Giovani Battista Piranesi, Public Domain
SKY10027850_070221

To Tofu

Contents

Chapter 1

For Whom? Why? And How?

I wrote this book for equity fundamental analysts and portfolio managers, present and future. I am addressing the reader directly: I am talking to *you*, the investor who is deeply in the weeds of the industry and the companies you cover, investigating possible mispricings or unjustified divergences in valuation between two companies. You, the reader, are obsessed with your work and want to be better at it. If you are reading this, and think, *that's me!*, rest assured: yes, it's probably you. You were the undergraduate in Chemical Engineering from Toronto who went from a summer job at a liquor store to founding an $8B hedge fund. The deeply thoughtful Norwegian pension fund manager who kept extending our meeting asking questions. The successful energy portfolio manager who interviewed me for my first hedge fund job, and the new college graduate from a large state university in Pennsylvania taking a job as an associate in a financials team.

I imagine that these readers are at different stages in their careers. Since the companies they cover are fundamentally different, they do think in different ways. But they all share a feature: they all have valuable trading ideas but realize that having good ideas is useless without the knowledge of how to turn them into money. This is the objective of portfolio construction and risk management: how to put together a portfolio of holdings that will be profitable over time and will survive adversities. This book is a short, incomplete guide toward investment enlightenment.

There is a second group of readers who will benefit from this book: the quantitative researchers who are, more and more, essential members of fundamental teams. There is not a strict separation between PMs and quantitative researchers. The quantitive researchers will find the appendix useful, if they want to implement programmatically the advanced tools the book describes.

1.1   What You Will Find Here

The book introduces a few themes, and then revisits them by adding details. You will learn how to:

1. *Separate stock-specific return drivers from the investment environment's return drivers;*
2. *Size your positions;*
3. *Understand your performance;*
4. *Measure and decompose risk;*
5. *Hedge the risk you don't want;*
6. *Use diversification to your advantage;*
7. *Manage losses;*
8. *Set your leverage.*

The approach I follow is to offer recommendations and best practices that are motivated by theory and confirmed by empirical evidence and successful practice. While I rely heavily on the framework of factor modeling, I believe that even a reader who does not currently have access to a risk model can still get a lot out of it. Day-to-day, several portfolio managers run very successful books without checking their factor risk decomposition every minute. The reason is that *they have converted insights into effective heuristics.* Wherever I can, I will flesh out these rules of thumb, and explain how and when they work.

1.2 Asterisks; Or, How to Read This Book

The mathematical requirements are minimal. Having taken an introductory course in Statistics should give the tools necessary to follow the text. Different readers have different objectives. Some want to get the gist of a book. Time is precious, only the thesis matters, its defense doesn't. *Gettysburg Address:* This new nation was conceived in Liberty, and dedicated to the proposition that all men are created equal. *Hamlet:* revenge is a futile pursuit. *Moby Dick: please*, don't hunt whales. To the *CliffsNotes*-oriented reader, to the secret agent perusing a book between Martinis: there is hope. Just read the sections that are not marked by a "★". Then there is the detail-oriented reader.

If you always collect all the trophies when playing a video game, or if you felt compelled to finish *War and Peace* in high school and didn't regret it: please read all the chapters and sections marked by "★", but skip the double-starred chapter "★★". You will learn the "Why" of things, not only the "How". These sections contain empirical tests and more advanced material and their results are not used in the remainder of the book. Finally, for the quantitative researcher and the risk manager, there is the double-starred appendix. Think of this as eleven on the volume knob of a guitar amplifier, as the "Chuck Norris Guide to Portfolio Construction." If you can read it, you should.

1.3 Acknowledgments

I thank Qontigo (formerly Axioma) for making available its US risk model; special thanks to Chris Canova and Sebastian Ceria. Samantha Enders, Purvi Patel, and Bill Falloon at Wiley guided the book composition from the first phone call to its publication. The following people read the book and provided corrections and feedback: Ashish Bajpai, Victor Bomers, Omer Cedar, Phil Durand, François Drouin, Ross Fabricant, Tom Fleming, Izabella Goldenberg, Ernesto Guridi, Dimitrios Margaritis, Chris Martin, Michael Medeiros, Gurraj Singh

Sangha, Ashutosh Singh, David Stemerman, Thomas Twiggs, Davide Vetrale, and Bernd Wuebben. I also owe much to people with whom I discussed – and from whom I learned about – several of these topics. Although they are too many to mention them all, Ravi Aggarwal, Brandon Haley, Gustav Rydbeck, Fabian Blohm, Costis Maglaras, Sai Muthialu, Vishal Soni and Samer Takriti, and, again, Sebastian Ceria have taught me most of what I know. All remaining errors are mine.

Chapter 2

The Problem: From Ideas to Profit

For those of you who are starting now, you are entering an industry in transition. If you could travel in time to 1995 and visit a portfolio manager's desk, you would have seem him or her using the same tools, processes and data they are using in 2020: Microsoft Excel, to model company earnings; a Bloomberg terminal; company-level models of earnings (also written in Excel), quarterly conferences where one meets with company executives. All of this is changing. Aside from the ever-present game of competition and imitation, two forces are moving the industry. The first is the availability of new data sources. "New", because storage and computational advances make it possible to collect and process unstructured, transactional data sets that were not collected before. And "available", because networking and cloud computing reduce dramatically the cost of consuming and managing these data. The second driving force is the transition of new analytical tools from *mathematics* to *technology*. Optimization, Factor Models, Machine Learning methods for supervised and unsupervised prediction: these were once advanced techniques that required expertise and relied on immature software prototypes. Now we have tools – technologies, really – that are robust, easy-to-use, powerful and free. Bloomberg and Excel are no longer sufficient, and with that, the toolkit that served the industry for so many years is suddenly incomplete. To meet the new challenges, fundamental teams are hiring "data scientists". Don't be fooled by the generic title. These are people who need to combine quantitative rigor and technical expertise with the investment process. Very often, they test new data sources; they run optimizations; they test hypotheses that the portfolio manager formulated. Ultimately, however, it is the portfolio manager who constructs the portfolio and supervises the action of the data scientist. The portfolio manager knows alphas, portfolio construction, risk management and data, and these are deeply connected. The success of a strategy is up to her competency and knowledge of these topics. A good portfolio manager can be – and should be! – a good risk manager, too. I believe it is possible to explain the basics of a systematic approach to portfolio construction without resorting to advanced mathematics and requiring much preexisting knowledge. This book is an elementary book in the sense that it assumes very little. I hope most readers will find in it something they already know, but that all readers will find something they did not know.

It seems inevitable that many books on this important subject must exist. In my years spent working as a quantitative researcher and consultant for the sell- and the buy-side, I have never been able to wholeheartedly recommend a book to my clients and colleagues that would help them in their endeavors. Like Italian art during the Renaissance, real-world finance works through a system of apprenticeship. Finance practitioners acquire most of their knowledge by doing and experiencing things. They talk and listen to risk-takers like themselves. They believe *portfolio managers* more than "managers" who have never managed a portfolio. They have a strong incentive not to share knowledge with outsiders, in order to protect their edge. All of this conspires against the existence of a good book on portfolio construction. Although the distance between professionals and academics is smaller in Finance than in other disciplines, it is still wide; the specific subject of portfolio management is covered by only a handful of journals.[1]

Summing up, there is no *master theory* yet of portfolio management. There are *problems* and *technologies* to solve in part these problems. Theories come and go; but a solution to a real problem is forever. As you explore portfolio management, you will find papers on optimization, position sizing, exploratory analysis of alternative data, timing of factors. Keep in mind the following maxim, which I paraphrase from a seminal paper on reproducible research:

> An article about the theory of portfolio management is not the scholarship itself, it is merely **advertising** of the scholarship.
> *[Buckheit and Donoho, 1995]*

Always look for simulation-based validations of a theory, and question the soundness of the assumptions in the simulation; and always look for empirical tests based on historical data, while being aware that these historical tests are most interesting when they show the limits of applicability of the theory, not when they confirm it [López de Prado, 2020].

Now, what are the problems?

2.1   How to Invest in Your Edge, and Hedge the Rest

Perhaps the simplest and deepest challenge is to understand the limits of your knowledge. If you develop a thesis with regard to the value of a company, you implicitly have a thesis on the peers of that company. All valuation judgements are relative. The question is, relative to what? The goal is to understand the drivers of pervasive returns, i.e., not of returns that we can forecast through deep investigation of a specific company, but rather that have a common explanatory factor;

---

[1] Among them, *The Journal of Portfolio Management, The Journal of Financial Data Science,* and the *Financial Analysts Journal.*

and then measure performance relative to those factors. There are at least two payoffs from following this process:

- The first is an improvement in the alpha research process. If you know what the environment is, then you know if a bet on a particular company carries with it unintended bets. Separating the stock from the environment gives you *clarity of thought.*
- The second is an improvement in the risk management process. If you know your environment, you can control your risk much more effectively; specifically, you can effectively reduce the environmental risk and keep only your intended bets; you can *hedge out what you don't know.*[2]

This subject is covered throughout the book, and is the main subject of Chapters 3, 4, and 5.

2.2   How to Size Your Positions

Once you have effectively estimated the true stock-specific return, your next problem is converting a thesis into an investment. It stands to reason that, the stronger the conviction, the larger the position should be. This leaves many questions unanswered. Is conviction the only variable? How does stock risk enter the sizing decision? What is the role played by the other stocks in the portfolio?

This is the subject of Chapter 6.

2.3   How to Learn from Your History

According to Plato, Socrates famously told the jury that sentenced him to death that "the unexamined life is not worth living". He was probably referring to portfolio managers. Billions of people happily live their unexamined yet worthy lives, but not many portfolio managers survive for long without examining their strategies.

---

[2] Joe Armstrong, a leading computer scientist and the inventor of the computer language Erlang, uses an effective metaphor for the lack of separation between the object of interest and its environment: *You wanted a banana but what you got was a gorilla holding the banana and the entire jungle* [Seibel, 2009].

If you want to remain among the (professionally) living, you must make a habit of periodically revisiting your decisions and learning from them. The life of the good portfolio manager is one marked by continuous self-doubt and adaptation. The distinctive features of a strategy's performance are stock selection, position sizing, and timing skills. The challenge is how to quantify them and improve upon them.

This is the subject of Chapter 8.

2.4   How to Trade Efficiently

Transaction costs play a crucial role in the viability of a trading strategy. Often, portfolio managers are not fully aware of the fact that these costs can eat up a substantial fraction of their revenues. As a result, they may over-trade, either by opening and closing positions more aggressively than needed, or by adjusting too often the size of a position over the lifetime of the trade. Earning events and other catalysts like product launches, drug approvals, sell-side upgrades/downgrades are an important source of revenue for fundamental PMs; how should one trade these events in order to maximize revenues inclusive of costs? Finally, what role should risk management play in event (and, in particular, earnings) trades? Positioning too early exposes the PM to unwanted risk in the days preceding the event.

This is the subject of Sections 8.2.1 and 8.3.

2.5   How to Limit Factor Risk

The output of your fundamental research changes continuously. The rules of your risk management process should not. They should be predictable, implementable, effective. These usually come in the form of limits: on your deployed capital, on your deployed portfolio risk, but also on less obvious dimensions of your strategy; for example, single-position maximum size is an important aspect of risk management. The challenge is to determine the rules that allow a manager to fully express her ideas while controlling risk.

This is the subject of Section 7.2.

2.6   How to Control Maximum Losses

An essential mandate of a manager is to protect capital. The Prime Directive, in almost everything, is to survive. A necessary condition for survival is not to exceed a loss threshold beyond which the future of the firm or of your strategy would be compromised. This is often implemented via explicit or implicit stop-loss policies. But how to set these policies? And how does the choice of a limit affect your performance?

This is the subject of Chapter 9.

2.7   How to Determine Your Leverage

This challenge is not faced by all portfolio managers. When they are working for a multi-PM platform, leverage decisions are the responsibility of the firm. However, a few independent investors do start their own hedge funds, and choosing a leverage that makes the firm viable, attractive to investors, and prudent is perhaps the most important decision they face.

This is the subject of Chapter 10.

2.8   How to Analyze New Sources of Data

New sources of data that go far beyond standard financial information become available every day. The portfolio manager faces the challenge of evaluating them, processing them and incorporating them into their investment process. The ability to transform data and extract value from them will become an important competitive advantage in the years to come. The range of methods available to an investor is as wide as the methods of Statistics, Machine Learning and Artificial Intelligence, and experimenting with them all is a daunting task. Are there ways to screen and learn from data so that the output is consistent with and complementary to your investment process?

This is the subject of Section 8.4.

Chapter 3

A Tour of Risk
and Performance

- *What will you learn here:* A very gentle introduction to factor models, starting with the simplest example of a model, which you probably already know. And how risk estimation, performance attribution and hedging can be performed using this simple approach.
- *Why do you need it:* Because the themes I introduce here will return over and over again throughout the book, from simple heuristics to advanced optimizations.
- *When will you need this:* Always. This will become your second nature. You will break the ice at cocktail parties mentioning how much risk decomposition helped you in your life.

11

3.1   Introduction

On July 3, 1884, the *Customer's Afternoon Letter* (owned by Dow Jones & Co.) began publishing the first stock index: a simple price average of nine transportation companies and two industrial ones. In 1886 it published the first Dow Jones Industrial Average. In 1889, the newspaper became *The Wall Street Journal*, and over time more indices were created. Indices provided a *benchmark* against which to compare one's investment; and they are a *summary* of the overall behavior of the market or of a specific sector. A typical benchmarking exercise: if we hold a stock, on any given day we first look at the overall market return, as provided by the index, and then we compute the out- or underperformance of the stock compared to the market. When we look at indices as market summaries, we implicitly know that they describe most, or at least some, of the stock returns for that market segment. In a very real way, having an index gives us a way to describe *performance* and *variation* of stock returns. Factor models capture these two intuitive facts, make it rigorous, and extend them in many directions.

A first extension aims to offer more flexibility in the relationship between stock and benchmark. For example, a cyclical stock in the financial sector like Synchrony Financial (ticker: SYF) moves more in sync (lame pun) with the market than, say, Walmart (ticker: WMT), a large, stable, defensive stock. Figure 3.1 bears this out. We take the daily returns of Synchrony and Wal-Mart and regress them against the daily returns of SPY.[1] The regression coefficient is denoted "beta". If the market returns an incremental 1%, the stock returns an incremental (beta) * (1%), everything else being equal. It is a measure of market sensitivity that differs from stock to stock. Figure 3.1 shows the regression of SYF daily returns against SP500 futures returns, for the period January 2, 2018, to December 31, 2019. Let us go with the assumption that we can estimate the true beta of a stock to the market; i.e., the estimation error of the beta doesn't really matter. Then a simple decomposition of market return + stock-specific return gives us a

---

[1] SPY is an ETF closely tracking the SP500 index.

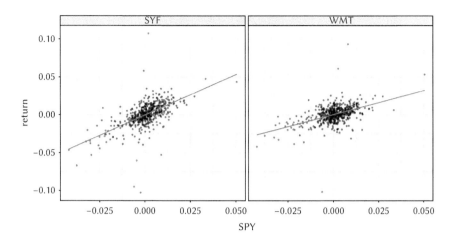

Figure 3.1   Linear regression of Synchrony's (SYF) and Wal-Mart's (WMT) daily returns against the SPY daily returns, using daily returns for the years 2018 and 2019.

great deal of information. On the benchmarking side, we now know what fraction of the return is attributable to the market. It may seem that SYF is outperforming the market in a bull market and Wal-Mart is underperforming. However, after decomposing returns, it may be the other way around: SYF is just a leveraged bet on the market, and after we remove the market contribution, SYF has underperformed, and WMT has outperformed. Another benefit from the linear relationship between market and stock returns is that it establishes a relationship among all stock returns. The market is the common link. For the overwhelming majority of stocks, the beta to the market is positive, but it can take values in a wide interval; several stocks exhibit betas higher than two. This relationship has implications for expected returns and risk as well. We will delve deeper into both later in this chapter. But before we proceed, we introduce a new term, "alpha". In your daily job, it's alpha that will pay your salary. Beta, on the other hand, can get you fired. This explains why so many portfolio managers have the symbol α tattooed on their bodies, while no one ever thought of getting a tattoo with the symbol β. Not even risk managers.

3.2   Alpha and Beta

Consider the regression line for SYF again. The complete formula for a linear regression includes an intercept and an error term, or residual. We write this explicitly. For a given stock,

$$
\begin{aligned}
r &= \alpha + \beta \times m + \epsilon \\
(return) &= (intercept) + (beta) \times (market) + (noise)
\end{aligned} \tag{3.1}
$$

Visually, this relationship is shown in Figure 3.2. We already introduced the term $\beta \times m$. This market component of the stock return is also called the *systematic* return of a stock. The first term on the left is the intercept α; it is a constant. When the market return is zero, the daily stock return is *in expectation* equal to alpha. No one observes expected returns, however. Even in the absence of market returns, the realized return of the stock would be $\alpha + \epsilon$. The last term is the "noise" around the stock return; it is also called *idiosyncratic* return of the stock. The terms *specific* and *residual* are also common, and we use all of them interchangeably. We would like to believe that this

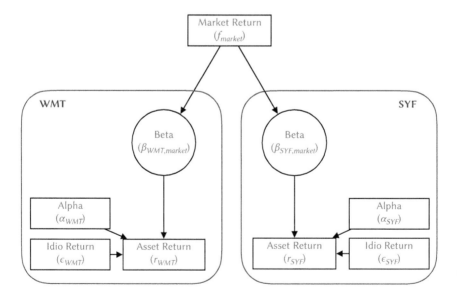

Figure 3.2   Flowchart illustrating the relationships between market, idio and asset returns, mediated by betas and offset by alphas. Market return times beta is added to alpha and idiosyncratic return to yield the total return.

nuisance term is specific to the company: every commonality among the stocks comes the beta and the market return. The simple model of Equation (3.1), with a single systematic source of return for all the stocks, is called a *single-factor model*.

The term $\alpha + \epsilon$ is only dependent on the company and nothing else. If that is the case, then the nuisance of many stocks diversifies away, a phenomenon that we will revisit many times in the following chapters. Alpha is the expected value of idiosyncratic return, and ϵ is the noise masking it. So, if we take the expectation of a stock return, what do we get? Alpha and Beta are constant, epsilon has expectation equal to zero, and the market return has a non-zero return.

$$(expected\ return) = (alpha) + (beta) \times (expected\ market\ return)$$

There is general agreement that accurately forecasting market returns is very difficult, and it is, at the very least, not in the mandate of a fundamental analyst. A macroeconomic investor may have an edge in forecasting the market; a fundamental one typically does not have a differentiated view. We can sketch the roles of various investment professionals as follows:

- To estimate α as accurately as possible is the job of the *fundamental investor*.
- To estimate β, identify the correct benchmarks m, and the returns ϵ is the job of the *quantitative risk manager*.
- To estimate the expected value of m (especially if the expectation changes over time) is the job of the *macroeconomic investor*.

But ultimately it is the job of the portfolio manager – who combines knowledge about mispricing with portfolio construction – to make use of relationship (3.1) to her own advantage.

3.3   Where Does Alpha Come From?

In the previous sections we used the example of SYF and WMT. We now analyze in more detail the historical estimates for SYF, using returns for year 2018. Table 3.1 shows the estimates and the 95% confidence interval. The error around the alpha estimate is much larger than the estimate itself, which is not the case for beta. Table 3.2 shows

Table 3.1 Parameter estimates for Synchrony's returns regressed against SP500 returns, 2018. Alphas are expressed in percentage annualized returns.

Parameter	Estimate	95% conf.interval
alpha (%)	−24	(−88, +8)
beta	1.02	(0.84, 1.20)

Table 3.2 Parameter estimates for Synchrony's returns regressed against SP500 returns, 2015–2019. Alphas are expressed in percentage annualized returns.

Year	Alpha (%)	Beta
2016	6	1.45
2017	−24	1.79
2018	−40	1.02
2019	16	1.15
2020	−19	1.69

the high degree of variability in the alphas, whereas the betas are relatively stable. This is the case for most stocks: estimates of alphas have large associated confidence intervals, and they seem to vary over time. You can't observe alpha directly, and you cannot estimate it easily from time series of returns. It is the job of the fundamental analyst to predict forward-looking alpha values based on deep fundamental research. *The ability to combine these alpha forecasts in non-trivial ways from a variety of sources and to process a large number of unstructured data is a competitive advantage of fundamental investing, and one that will not go away soon.* We list some of data sources and processes involved in the alpha generation process.

- *Valuation Analysis.* This differentiated view comes from a company business model whose data are coming primarily from Cash Flow Statements, Balance Sheets (Statements of Financial Positions), Income Statements and Stakeholder Equity Statements. It is complemented by macroeconomic data affecting the production function of the company as well as demand for its products and services. This is the domain of fundamental analysis [T. Koller and Wessels, 2015] and affects both short-term forecasts, e.g., earnings or the event of a sell-side analyst downgrading or upgrading a recommendation, and long-term forecast, such as the potential long-term unsuitability of a business.

- *Alternative Data.* Enabled by the availability of transactional data (e.g., credit card transactions) and environmental data (such as satellite imaging), these data complement fundamental analysis and give short-term information about demand, supply, costs, and potential risks. A textbook account of alternative data in finance is [Denev and Amin, 2020]; a reference for data sources, published by J.P. Morgan, is [Kolanovic and Krishnamachari, 2017].
- *Sentiment Analysis.* This can be interpreted as the subset of alternative data that gives information about demand that is a function of the consumer's expectations of the future state of the economy. Common macroeconomic time series are Conference Board's Consumer Confidence Index, the University of Michigan's Survey of Consumers, and the Purchasing Managers' Index. At the company level, it is possible to gain information from unstructured data [Loughran and McDonald, 2016].
- *Corporate Access.* Interactions between analysts and company managers occur on a quarterly basis. Although these communications are public information, fundamental analysts can make the best use of them by comparing to previous quarter guidance and by linking them to the vast information accumulated by the analyst on that company.
- *Liquidity.* A company may enter or exit the composition of an index, may issue a secondary offering, or may go through the expiration of a stock lock-up period. All these events affect demand for the stock at a point in time. Although fundamental investors don't have an edge in these events, they take them into account nonetheless.
- *Crowding.* It's not only the analyst's thesis about a company that matters, but what is the thesis with respect to the consensus among informed investors and motivated but nonprofessional investors acting in a coordinated way. It is possible, to some extent, to measure this consensus; Section 5.2 is dedicated to this issue. Consensus measures help the analyst gauge the originality of her fundamental thesis, and the risk associated to taking position in a stock that may be enjoying growing popularity, but also fall quickly out of favor with a broad investing base.

3.4   Estimate Risk in Advance

The "stock return = market + idio" decomposition is about *returns*. But it is also a decomposition of *risk*. Returns are easy to define,[2] but risk is not. Before taking a risk definition for granted, it's worth devoting some time to the many meanings of the term.

3.4.1   *What Is Risk?*

"To risk" comes from the Italian verb *risicare* [Bernstein, 1996], as in the old proverb *chi non risica non rosica*: "those who don't take risk don't eat", which illustrates that you don't need to have a PhD to understand the trade-off between risk and return. When it comes to actually defining risk, opinions differ wildly. A deep value investor with little quantitative training may answer that risk is "the possibility of a permanent loss of capital", which sounds great until you try to determine what "permanent loss of capital" means. A company going bankrupt? Our investors withdrawing their capital from our fund? If our losses are large enough, our fund may be unable to meet its funding obligations. In this case, we would be forced to liquidate part of the portfolio or even to turn our entire portfolio over to our prime broker counterpart, another permanent loss of capital. And over what time horizon? In the long run we are all dead anyway. There is a nugget of truth in this definition, though. Risk is associated to the probability of losses large enough to disrupt our ability to invest. I am assuming you agree that is an acceptable definition of risk. But how to quantify the probability of a large loss? First, we need a probability distribution of losses; second, we need to set a limit on the loss, and our tolerance that it occurs. The first task is much harder than the second. To address it, we must have a good model of asset returns, especially in times of stress. This is not specific to fundamental investors: large financial institutions, like banks or insurers, face the same problem. In their case, a large loss impairs their ability to function or damages their reputation. Their problem is complicated by the fact that their portfolios are made of assets and liability claims that behave very

---

[2] Actually, not that easy. See the notes at the end of this chapter for more details on this topic.

differently from each other. The case of equities, however, is easier for two reasons. The first one is the relative simplicity of a cash security: a fractional ownership contract. The second one is that, if enough care is put into the models, the factor and idiosyncratic returns are sufficiently well-behaved, in the sense that their standard deviations:

1. are finite, as opposed to infinite, which could in principle be the case;
2. can be estimated, as opposed to being nonestimable because they are too noisy;
3. are the only statistics of interest, because higher-order statistics of returns, like skewness and kurtosis, cannot be estimated.[3]

These facts are *mostly* true, but far from obvious! Standard deviations are almost surely finite, are not straightforward to estimate, and most likely statistics more complex than the standard deviation are essentially not-estimable. Moreover, it is essential to have an understanding of the properties of returns for investment purposes, and for these reasons this book dedicates a full chapter to the statistical properties of returns. For this chapter's purposes, we take advantage of the fact that there are two quantities of paramount interest: the mean, which measured the *centrality* of returns, or their center of gravity; and the standard deviation, which measures the dispersion of returns around the mean. In finance, the standard deviation of a stock's returns is also referred to as *volatility*. You can hear that Wal-Mart has a 1% daily volatility. This means that Wal-Mart's daily returns have a 1% standard deviation.[4] With mean and volatility you can estimate losses; for example, we will use these statistics in Chapter 10. Oftentimes, we assume that returns are normally distributed. This is an optimistic assumption, but it provides a useful reference point, in the sense that changes in volatility estimations roughly correspond to changes in losses that could be experienced with a given probability. A loss of minus one standard deviation or more from the expected return occurs with a probability of about 16%. In one year (or 252 trading days), you can expect 40 days with such returns. A loss of

---

[3] See the surveys by Gabaix [2009], Cont [2001] and references therein.
[4] This does not mean that the average absolute size of returns is 1%; see the FAQ chapter for an explanation.

Table 3.3 Probabilities of occurrence of rare events under the normal distribution from "one sigma" event up to "three sigma".

std. deviations	Probability (%)	Events/year	Events/five yrs
−1.0	15.87	40	200
−2.0	2.28	6	29
−2.5	0.62	2	8
−3.0	0.13	0	2

minus two standard deviations or more occurs with probability 2.3%. Table 3.3 presents some numerical examples. The volatility of a stock, or of a portfolio, is the yardstick that allows us to measure and compare risk. The daily returns of a single asset are not normally distributed; taking it one step up in mathematical sophistication, they are not even log-normally distributed. However, based on its recent history, you can estimate its volatility reasonably well; and given its volatility, you can formulate a reasonable estimate of extreme losses. For a model of reality to be useful, it is sufficient that it work better than the alternative; certainly for equity returns there are no alternatives to factor models that are obviously better, and risk models do work well to perform a wide range of functions, and in a wide range of market regimes. Where we believe they fall short – and every model falls short! – we'll caution you.

3.4.2 Measuring Risk and Performance

The first use of risk models is for risk management. The questions we are asking are:

- What is the risk (i.e., the volatility) of my current portfolio?
- Where does the risk come from?
- How does the risk change as my portfolio changes?

We are going to answer them by proceeding in small steps. Start with the risk of a single stock. The risk model gives the pieces of information about Synchrony shown[5] in Table 3.4: What is the daily

---

[5] The Net Market Value, or NMV, is the signed dollar holding value of security held in a portfolio.

Table 3.4 Synchrony's risk parameters for the year 2019.

Field	Value (%)
Beta	1.2
Daily Market Vol (%)	0.8
Daily Idio Vol (%)	1.3
Net Market Value	$10M

volatility of owning $10M of SYF stocks? Recall that for Synchrony, and any other stock, the return formula is

$$r = \alpha + \beta \times m + \epsilon$$

We want to compute the volatility of Synchrony's stock return, vol(r). The alpha term is a constant, while the terms $\beta \times m$ and ϵ are random. The constant α does not contribute to volatility, but the two random terms do. What is the volatility of the sum of two random variables? The square of the volatility (or standard deviation) is also called the *variance* of a random variable. You may remember from a Statistics or Probability class that the variance of the sum of two independent random variables is equal to the sum of their variances. This is easier to show in pictures, because it is nothing else than Pythagoras's Theorem! The volatilities of two random variables are the two legs of a right triangle. The volatility of their sum is equal to the length of the hypotenuse; see Figure 3.3.

Now, we can apply this formula to Synchrony. The volatility of the market term is

$$\$10M \times 1.2 \times 0.8\% = \$96K$$

The idiosyncratic volatility is

$$\$10M \times 1.3\% = \$130K$$

The dollar variance of Synchrony returns is $96^2 + 130^2 = 26116K^2$ and finally the volatility is $162K.

I hope I bored you with this calculation, because *it is boring*. But this is a back-of-the-envelope calculation that helps for many tasks. For example: you can pull SYF and SP500 returns from a website

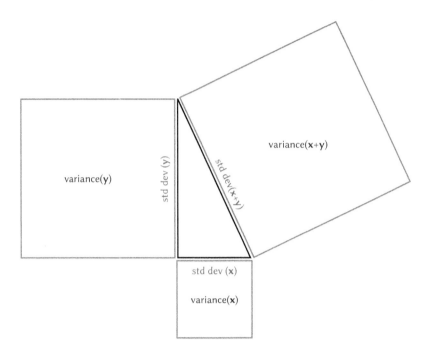

Figure 3.3   The variance of the sum of two independent random variables is equal to the sum to the variances of the two random variables. You can interpret the standard deviations as sides of a right triangle.

or Bloomberg for the past year, estimate their vols, then perform a quick regression in Excel to estimate the beta of SYF to SP500 and then use the same calculation above to derive the idiosyncratic vol (do it!). Yes, there is a Bloomberg function for that (BETA <GO>), and yes, even Yahoo Finance reports the trailing 3-year beta. But suppose that you don't want a three-year beta. Or suppose that you don't want to include a certain date range in SYF returns, for example, the day of an idiosyncratic event that resulted in a one-off large return, and is not representative of the future volatility of the stock. There are many valid reasons for wanting to customize the estimation of vols and betas. Once you have understood the principle, you are the master of your own destiny, even if you pull the data from a commercial model.

Now that we have understood the risk decomposition of a single stock into market and idio, let's extend to a whole portfolio. The parameters from the risk model and the portfolio are in Table 3.5.

Table 3.5 Synchrony, Wal-Mart and SP500 risk parameters, together with holdings for each asset.

Field	SYF	WMT	SPY
Beta	1.2	0.7	1
Daily Market Vol (%)			1.4
Daily Idio Vol (%)	1.2	0.5	0.0
Net Market Value	$10M	$5M	$10M

The daily PnL ("Profit and Loss") of the portfolio is defined as the sum of the holdings times their respective returns:

$$\text{PnL}_{\text{port}} = \text{NMV}_{\text{SYF}} \times r_{\text{SYF}} + \text{NMV}_{\text{WMT}} \times r_{\text{WMT}} + \text{NMV}_{\text{SPY}} \times r_{\text{SPY}}$$

Now, we can use Equation (3.1) to replace returns with their components, and rearrange the terms:

$$\text{PnL}_{\text{port}} = (\text{NMV}_{\text{SYF}} \times \beta_{\text{SYF}} + \text{NMV}_{\text{WMT}} \times \beta_{\text{WMT}} + \text{NMV}_{\text{SPY}} \times \beta_{\text{SPY}})m \tag{3.2}$$

(market contribution)

$$+ (\text{NMV}_{\text{SYF}} \times \epsilon_{\text{SYF}} + \text{NMV}_{\text{WMT}} \times \epsilon_{\text{WMT}} + \text{NMV}_{\text{SPY}} \times \epsilon_{\text{SPY}})$$

(idiosyncratic contribution)

The *performance* of the portfolio can be split into the contribution of two terms: a market term and an idiosyncratic one. This is a simple example of *performance attribution.*

The beta of the portfolio is $1.2 \times \$10M + 0.7 \times \$5M + 1 \times \$10M = \$25.5M$. The important thing to notice is that the beta of the portfolio is the sum of the betas of the individual holdings. This overall portfolio beta is expressed in dollars, and usually is called the dollar beta of the portfolio. This dollar beta, multiplied by the market return m, gives the contribution of the market to the portfolio PnL. The daily volatility of the portfolio deriving from the market is

$$(\textit{portfolio market volatility}) = (\textit{portfolio dollar beta})$$
$$\times (\textit{market volatility})$$
$$= \$25.5M \times 1.4\% = \$36K$$

An alternative way to quote the beta of a portfolio is in *percentage beta*, which is defined as the dollar beta divided by the net market value of the portfolio. If we netted out our positions, the percentage beta is the dollar beta per unit of dollar held long in the portfolio.[6] In our case the percentage beta is $25.5M/$25M \simeq 1.0$.

The other term is the idiosyncratic PnL. The volatility of the idiosyncratic PnL of the portfolio is the sum of three terms. As in the case of two variables, the variance of the sum is the sum of the variances:

$$(\textit{portfolio idio variance}) = (\text{NMV}_{\text{SYF}} \times \text{vol}_{\text{SYF}})^2$$
$$+ (\text{NMV}_{\text{WMT}} \times \text{vol}_{\text{WMT}})^2$$
$$+ (\text{NMV}_{\text{SPY}} \times \text{vol}_{\text{SPY}})^2$$

And the volatility is

$$(\textit{portfolio idio volatility}) = \sqrt{(10 \times 1.2)^2 + (5 \times 0.5)^2} = \$122\text{K}$$

Finally, the variance of the portfolio is the sum of the variances, because idio and market returns are independent of each other. The volatility is the square root:

$$(\textit{portfolio total volatility}) = \sqrt{36^2 + 122^2} = \$127\text{K}$$

The procedure is described in Procedure Box 3.1. Let us go through another simple example.

Procedure 3.1 Compute the volatility of a portfolio.

---

1. Compute the dollar betas for the individual positions;
2. Compute the dollar portfolio beta as the sum of the individual betas;
3. Compute the market component of the volatility as *(portfolio beta) × (market volatility)*;
4. Compute the dollar idio volatility as the square root of the sum of the squared dollar volatilities.

---

[6] This definition makes sense only for assets with a non-zero portfolio NMV, and typically a positive NMV, i.e., for net-long portfolios.

Table 3.6 Portfolio example, with increasing number of stocks. Each stock has unit beta. The daily stocks' idio vol and market vol are both 1%.

# Stocks	Idio Vol ($)	Market Vol ($)	Idio Var (% tot)
1	1M	1M	50
10	316K	1M	9.09
100	100K	1M	0.99
1000	31.6K	1M	0.01

Say that you consider four long-only portfolios, each one with $100M of market value. The first one has one stock, the second one has ten stocks, the third has 100 stocks, the fourth one has 1000 stocks. Each stock has beta 1, and a daily idio vol of 1%. The market also has a daily vol of 1%. These are made-up numbers of course, but they simplify the calculation, and real portfolios are not that far from these values. What are the idio and market components of these portfolios? Table 3.6 has the numbers.[7]

Given this example, you can now understand better why SPY has zero percentage idio volatility in Table 3.5. The SPY is a long-only portfolio of 500 stocks. Each stock in the portfolio has a positive beta. As a percentage of the total risk, the idiosyncratic risk is very small, and is usually approximated to zero.

3.5 First Steps in Risk Decomposition

This very simple decomposition already has very powerful implications. Volatility either comes from a systematic source or a stock-specific one. Where does your skill lie? In going long or short the market, or rather in going long or short the company-specific returns? One attractive feature of being long the market is that its risk is accompanied by positive expected returns. The inflation-adjusted annualized historical return of the S&P 500 from 1926 (the inception year of the index) to 2018 is 7%; so it may seem a good idea to have a positive beta to the market. Indeed, a sizable fraction of the global

---

[7] If you want to understand the reason why the idiosyncratic volatility of a diversified, long-only portfolio comprised of many stock is low, you can read the next-to-last question in the Risk FAQ (Section 4.2).

assets under management are actively managed funds that track an index. This means that the portfolio has a positive percentage beta, often equal to 1, and a certain budget of volatility allowed to run in idiosyncratic PnL, sometimes called the tracking error. For example, our previous portfolio in Table 3.5 has a tracking dollar vol of $1.9M, or, in percentage of the portfolio's NMV, a 7.8% tracking error.[8] Compared to commercial products, this is a relatively high value. Tracking errors range from 0% (i.e., a "passive" fund tracking the market) to 6 or 7%, which is not hard to achieve when the portfolio consists of hundreds of securities rather than three. One less attractive feature of carrying beta in your portfolio is that it is harder and harder to justify to investors. The principals who entrusted their capital to you also see the alpha-beta decomposition; and they usually have very inexpensive ways to invest in the market, either by buying e-mini SP futures, or by buying a low-expense ratio ETF like SPY, or by investing in a passive fund like Vanguard's Total Stock Market Index Fund. This decomposition, which is useful to you to understand your return, is available to them as well, and the beta component is easy to replicate. Therefore, if you still want to keep a significant beta in your portfolio, you better have a good argument. We will revisit one such argument in Chapter 8, which is devoted to performance. For the time being, it suffices to point out two facts. The first one is that any argument in favor of conflating beta and alpha is weaker than the simple argument in favor of decomposing them. Secondly, that it is easy to *remove* the market component from a portfolio. This is the subject of the next section.

3.6   Simple Hedging

We revisit the example portfolio in Table 3.5. We had a portfolio with a large amount of market risk, but we also have $6.7M of idiosyncratic risk coming from SYF and WMT. In addition, we have high conviction

---

[8] The annualized tracking vol is approximately $0.122M \times \sqrt{252} \simeq \$1.9M$. The annualization calculation is explained later, in Section 4.2. You can ignore the details of the calculation on a first reading.

that these two stocks will have returns in excess of the market in the next quarter, whereas we have very little idea of the direction of the market over the same time horizon. We can express this by saying that we have an *edge* in our specific stock selections, but not in the market. Even if we did not hold any SPY, we would risk marring our good insight about the underpriced SYF and WMT stock. A large market drawdown can result in negative returns for the portfolio. If we seek absolute returns from our portfolio, this may not be a wise choice. We can remedy this by taking a *short* position in SPY. We borrow the shares from an existing owner and we sell them at the market price. At some point in the future, we *cover* the position by purchasing the shares at the market price and returning them to their owner. Shorting has costs and risk. We pay a "borrow rate" to the lender, which can be high if the stocks are hard to find (or *locate*). In addition, shorted stocks can be recalled by the original owner if she wants to sell them, forcing us to cover the stock earlier than anticipated.[9] By shorting SPY, we reduce the beta exposure of the portfolio. The dollar beta for SYF is $12M; for WMT it is $2.5M. The total dollar beta is $25.5m. SPY has a beta of 1. If we sell the entire SPY position and further short $15.5M, the total beta of the portfolio is zero. The market component of the portfolio volatility is proportional to its dollar beta, and is therefore zero. And the idiosyncratic risk of the portfolio? It has not changed, because SPY has no idio volatility (to a very good approximation). The summary statistics of the hedged portfolio are in Table 3.7. The procedure is described in Procedure Box 3.2.

Table 3.7   Synchrony, Wal-Mart and SP500 risk parameters, together with holdings for each asset for a market-hedged portfolio.

Field	SYF	WMT	SPY
Beta	1.2	0.5	1
Daily Market Vol (%)			1.4
Daily Idio Vol (%)	1.2	0.7	0.0
Net Market Value ($M)	10	5	−15.5

---

[9] In this event, the Prime Broker usually attempts to locate new stocks before forcing covering the position.

Procedure 3.2 Compute the market hedge of a portfolio.

---

1. Compute the dollar betas for the individual positions of the unhedged portfolio;
2. Compute the dollar portfolio beta as the sum of the individual betas;
3. Compute the market hedge NMV, whose value is equal to the opposite of the portfolio beta.

This is perhaps the simplest possible hedging scenario one may imagine, and yet it is applied daily to portfolios with Gross Market Values[10] of hundreds of billions of dollars. These portfolios are usually long-short, but they still do carry beta exposures, which are computed and hedged several times a day using liquid instruments like equity futures. In Chapter 6 we will expand the concept in several directions.

3.7   Separation of Concerns

We saw that a simple factor model enables you to do performance attribution, risk decomposition and hedging. These three tasks are tightly connected. If from risk decomposition you can detect that market risk is large, then it is more likely that a substantial fraction of your PnL is attributable to market returns, and this also means that this market risk can be completely hedged, and that the market-originated PnL can be eliminated. Behind it all, this framework enables you to see at work a fundamental design principle: *separation of concerns* [Dijkstra, 1982]. Disparate activities like building a car, writing the code for a video game or managing a portfolio have one thing in common: they are tasks that require solving many problems at once. If we had to address them all at once, we would likely build a Ford Pinto,[11] release

---

[10] The Gross Market Value (GMV) of a stock is the absolute value of the Net Market Value. The GMV of a portfolio is the sum of the GMVs of the individual positions.

[11] A car so well engineered that it managed to be ugly and burst into flames in a low-speed collision.

Duke Nukem Forever[12] or be forced to shut down in record time. In order to control complexity, we need to identify smaller, simpler parts of the system; we need to separate them and solve the issues related to them; and finally we have to put them back together with little effort. Modularization, Encapsulation, and Composition. Factor models allow us to separate factor idiosyncratic returns. In the process, they help us separate unwanted risk and performance from intentional risk and performance. When we size our positions, we do so to capture the sources of returns that are specific to a firm. We have a clean way to address the unwanted risk, via hodging. Even better, in the following chapters you will learn about factors and their interpretation, so that the subsystem that constitutes "unwanted risk" can give you context about the investing environment. And this environment can be further decomposed in smaller components, such as country, industry and style risks, which we will cover in the following chapters.

3.8   Takeaway Messages

Risk models serve four main purposes:

1. *Risk Measurement:* Estimate the volatility of a portfolio, and from this estimate, the probability of the loss exceeding a certain threshold.
2. *Risk Decomposition:* The risk comes either from common sources (systematic component) or stock-specific sources.
3. *Performance Attribution:* Systematic and idiosyncratic sources of returns determine also the performance, and the entire performance of a book through time can be attributed to a combination of both.
4. *Hedging:* Once the systematic source of risk has been identified, it can be removed without affecting the idiosyncratic sources of return (and risk).

---

[12] Famously announced in 1997, it was released in 2011. And it was still an awful game.

Chapter 4

An Introduction
to Multi-Factor Models

- *What will you learn here:* What are multi-factor risk models; how many different types of models are there; and how are they estimated? Most importantly, how do they allow you to separate two worlds: the world of factors from that of company-specific returns?
- *Why does this matter:* Because it is the skeleton that supports the whole thing. Even if you do not see it, it is there and it is essential.
- *When will you need this:* Always and never. Always, because you will consume its byproduct daily; (almost) never, because you won't have to think about "factor portfolios", or cross-sectional regressions unless you really miss them.

4.1 From One Factor to Many

We have seen that alphas do not come from straightforward regressions. What about betas? Is the market beta the beta to end all betas? It turns out that this is just the beginning of the story. The single-beta factor model was proposed independently by Lintner and Mossin, and Sharpe, who gave it the now-standard name Capital Asset Pricing Model (CAPM), in the mid-1960s. It was immediately put to the test. Initial empirical studies confirmed the model [Black et al., 1972; Fama and MacBeth, 1973]. In the mid-1970s, three separate contributions by young researchers set the stage for a second revolution. First, Stephen Ross, then an assistant professor at Yale, extended the CAPM. His starting point is to assume that there is a small number of factors, compared to the number of assets, which act on the returns, not unlike the CAPM. Compare Figure 4.1 to Figure 3.2.

$$r = \alpha + \beta^1 \times f_1 + \ldots + \beta^m \times f_m + \epsilon \qquad (4.1)$$

The betas in the Eq. (4.1) are termed *loadings* of a specific stock to a factor; this term is borrowed from the statistics literature on factor

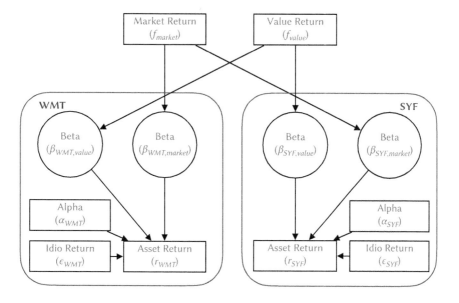

Figure 4.1 Analogous to Figure 3.2 but for two factors.

models. That same year, Barr Rosenberg (then an associate professor at Berkeley) and Vinay Marathe [Rosenberg and Marathe, 1976] proposed that loadings be *characteristics* of a stock. For example, we could create a financial ratio like cash flow to price (a profitability measure) for each company, and use it as a factor loading. The interpretation of the "cash flow to price" return then is similar to that of the market: when this return is positive, companies with high ratios have, everything else being equal, higher expected returns than companies with low ratios. There is one important difference, though: in the case of the CAPM, we could observe the market factor. Not so for the profitability factor. It is not a macroeconomic time series, nor a portfolio. No one "sees" this factor. However, there is a way around this problem. The basic idea is simple and powerful. We can build a "profitability" portfolio, i.e., a portfolio whose returns are very similar to the true profitability return. We will revisit this idea in this book, because it has applications for fundamental investors, too.

The last leg of the multi-factor stool came from Chicago. A Swiss assistant professor, Rolf Banz, then just starting at Northwestern, published part of his thesis [Banz, 1981]. This time, the challenge to the CAPM was empirical: there was evidence that small-cap stocks outperformed large-cap stocks; i.e., stocks exhibited different expected returns based on an attribute different than the market beta: market capitalization. Instead of one factor, we have at least two: a market-based one and a market-cap-based one. The formula giving the return of a stock now looks like this,

$$r = \alpha + \beta^M r^M + \beta^{BMS} r^{BMS} + \epsilon$$

where "M" stands for "Market" and "BMS" stands for "Big Minus Small". The study was exceptionally influential.[1] The papers of Ross and Banz together have more academic citations than there are seats in an average soccer stadium. Barr's papers are not nearly as cited, but that is because Rosenberg soon left academia to start a number of successful companies: Barra (now MSCI), Barclays Global Investors (now part of Blackrock), and AXA Rosenberg. Ross and

---

[1] In an interesting development, this original challenge was itself challenged! Today, the original "size effect" is not considered a real effect. A survey is [Alquist et al., 2018].

Banz had successful investment careers as well. The commercial factor models sold by Barra introduced conceptual innovations, but also broke a technological barrier. In 1980, there were approximately 5,000 listed companies in the US; a covariance matrix of these assets has approximately $(5000 \times 5000)/2$ distinct estimates.[2] That is 12.5M numbers, or about 50MB of data after compression. Even if the matrix had been generated once a month (daily models are an invention of the new millennium), that would have been a lot of data to transfer at a rate of a few KB/sec. Alternatively, you would have had to send a large pizza tape, or *a lot* of floppy disks to your clients. But with a reasonable model, say of 50 factors, the data size of the model would have been 50x smaller: by far the large piece of data would have been the stocks' characteristics, many of which are 0/1 numbers. Commercialization became possible.

Since 1981, there has been an explosion of factors explaining equity returns. Moreover, the factor approach has been applied successfully to other asset classes like government bonds and corporate credit. How are the factors discovered? And where do the betas come from? There are broadly three ways to attack this problem and we already saw two of them:

1. *The time-series approach.* We are surrounded by time-series data. Macroeconomic indicators, inflation, interest rates, economic growth, employment data, business cycle indicators. Economic sentiment data, like consumer confidence. Then, there are detailed economic activity data: same-store sales; purchasing manager indices; or international vs. domestic activity. Commodity prices (esp. oil) also affect economic activity. All of these data are factor candidates. You estimate the sensitivity (or beta) of a stock to these factors by performing a time-series regression of the stock return to the time series. The factor returns (the time series) are known; the betas are derived using asset and factor returns.

2. *The fundamental approach.* This is the method pioneered by Barr Rosenberg. Each stock has characteristics. These characteristics describe the company and its returns. We have to identify the relevant characteristics, which serve as the betas of the model. We

---

[2] The matrix is symmetric, so you only need the top-right half of the matrix.

then need to populate these fields for every stock, every characteristic, and every period. In this model, the betas are the primitive
information, the factor returns are derived: given the betas and the
asset returns, you can estimate the factor returns.

3. *The statistical approach.* In this method, you are only given the
   time series of asset returns. Both the beta and the factor returns
   are estimated using the asset returns alone. This may seem magi-
   cal. Don't we need one or the other? The approach side-steps the
   problem by choosing betas and returns so as to describe most of
   the variation in the asset returns.

Each of these approaches has its merits and drawbacks, so that
none of them dominates all of the others. In fact, risk models often
use a mix of two or even three of them. The characteristic model
has the benefit of being interpretable by the managers. The industry
to which a company belongs is more like a simple yes/no flag
than a time-series beta to an "industry return". These models can
be extended with new characteristics and perform quite well in
practical applications. Because of these two decisive advantages the
fundamental (or characteristic) method is by far the most used model
by fundamental managers. Yet, the time series model is necessary
whenever the data are in the form of time series. In this case, we
estimate time series betas. Time-series-based models are more popular in the academic literature than in the real world, both because
of interpretability and performance concern. Time-series betas are
however used as additional characteristics in fundamental models.
Finally, statistical models have the least data requirement of all; and
they have comparable performance for volatility prediction. However,
beyond the first factor (or, at most, the second one), they are difficult
to interpret. In equity models, factors have hardly any meaning,
aside from the first one, which can be viewed as a market factor. And
yet, statistical models occasionally find applications for fundamental
managers, too. They are used as "second opinions", and also to check
whether the base model (which is almost always a fundamental one)
is missing some systematic source of risk. We summarize the pros
and cons of the three approaches in Table 4.1. In the remainder of this
chapter, I will focus on fundamental models, since they matter to you
the most. And of their many aspects (estimation, performance, and

Table 4.1 Comparison of different approaches to modeling risk.

Model	Data Needs	Performance	Interpretability
Time Series	Medium	Low	Medium-High
Fundamental	High	High	High
Statistical	Low	High	Low

historical development) I will cover just two, but, in my opinion, the most important for you:

- First, I provide a list of the most important factors, their interpretation, and why they matter to you. On each of these factors, tens of papers have been written, with explanations, variants and tests. I will skim the surface, and point to a few books that contain a more thorough discussion.
- Second, I believe it's useful to peek inside the black box of model estimation. As a fundamental investor, you will never estimate a model in your life; as a human, you will never paint a Van Gogh, or design a turbine, either, but you will appreciate them more by understanding the design principles that guided their creation. You already know that the inputs to the model are the stock characteristics (for each stock) and the asset returns. The output are many: factor returns, idiosyncratic returns, idiosyncratic volatilities, factor covariances...what are these things, and where do they come from is the subject of the next section.

4.2 ★Frequently Asked Questions About Risk

This section collects several common questions and "how-tos" for risk models. These questions really do come up all the time. You can skip it on a first reading, but whenever you have a practical question or doubt, please check this section first.

Q: *How can two models with different versions of the factors (e.g., z-scored vs. raw) be different for specific factors and equivalent in the aggregate?*

A: On an intuitive level, the characteristics in the two models contain the same information, so it makes sense that operationally they are equivalent. On a more rigorous level, try the following experiment in Excel: perform a univariate linear regression (i.e., one dependent variable, one independent variable, and the intercept). Take note of the R-squared of the regression. Now, replace the first variable by its centered version and repeat the regression. You will see that the regression coefficients have changed, but the R-squared hasn't. The predictive power of the regression doesn't change if you mix and match the variables. The same principle is at work in a factor model.

Q: *What is the unit of measure of the loadings? Of the exposures? Of the portfolio volatility?*

A: Loadings are pure, dimensionless numbers. Exposures are numbers times positions in local currency, so they are in currency units. Volatility is in currency *or* in percentages. A $10M annualized volatility means that the annual range of variation of the portfolio is $10M; this number is independent of the Gross Market Value of the portfolio. An annualized volatility of 10% for a portfolio with a gross market value of $1B means that the annual range of variation is 10% × $1B, or $100M.

Q: *How do I convert the annualized volatility of a portfolio into a weekly or a monthly volatility?*

A: Recall that the variances of independent random variable sum up. The annual variance of a portfolio is the sum of the weekly variances: variance(yearly) = variance(week 1) + variance(week 2) + ... + variance(week 52) = 52 × variance(weekly). The volatility is the square root of the variance, therefore

$$(yearly\ volatility) = \sqrt{52} \times (weekly\ volatility)$$

The weekly volatility is the annual volatility divided by $\sqrt{52}$. There are approximately 252 trading days in a year; by a similar reasoning, the daily volatility is the annual volatility divided by $\sqrt{252}$. Formulas for monthly, quarterly or multi-year vol are derived similarly.

Q: *Is the daily volatility equal to the average absolute daily return?*

A: No. If we assume that a return r is normally distributed with standard deviation σ and mean zero, the absolute return follows the distribution of a *folded normal distribution.* The expected value is given by [Leone et al., 1961] by

$$(average\ absolute\ daily\ return) = \sqrt{\frac{2}{\pi}} \times (daily\ volatility)$$

$$\simeq 0.8 \times (daily\ volatility)$$

so it is slightly smaller than the daily volatility. In practice, since we saw that both factor returns and idiosyncratic returns are heavy-tailed, the average absolute daily return is smaller than 80% of the daily volatility.

Q: *Why can't I estimate expected returns from historical returns using some law of large numbers? If I use hourly returns instead of daily returns to increase the size of my dataset, can I get a more accurate estimate?*

A: You can't hope to increase the accuracy of your historical estimates from historical data. Say that the returns of a stock are normally distributed, have expected annualized returns α and annualized volatility equal to σ. If you split one year in n intervals (252 for daily returns; 1640 for hourly returns; 9800 for 10-minute returns), then the expected return in one period is α/n and the volatility is $\sigma/\sqrt{n}$ (as we have seen from the previous question about volatility scaling). When you take the average of the n returns, the expected value of the per-period return is α/n; the standard error of the estimate is equal to the standard error of the return around the mean (i.e., $\sigma/\sqrt{n}$) divided by the square root of the number of observations, as you may recall from introductory statistics. Hence the estimation error is

$$(\sigma/\sqrt{n})/\sqrt{n} = \sigma/n$$

So our 95% confidence interval for the expected return is

$$\frac{\alpha}{n} \pm 1.96\frac{\sigma}{n} = \frac{1}{n}(\alpha \pm 1.96\sigma)$$

The greater the value of n, the smaller the value, as expected. But the relative size of the error doesn't depend on n! The signal-to-noise ratio, defined as the ratio of the expected value of the estimate to its standard error, is α/σ; and it is reasonable to expect α to be much smaller than σ. Even if we have a very large number of observations, the accuracy does not improve. The problem is that, as we increase the number of observations n, we have to estimate a fainter signal: not α, but α/n.

Q: *Your model predicts a volatility that is 50% my current realized volatility. But I have been given by my hedge fund a risk budget based on predicted volatility. It is very difficult for me to make money!*

A: Usually this is occurring in the aftermath of a large volatility event: think September 2008, November 2016, or March 2020. Volatility models still rely on recent history; and if history shows a big spike in returns, it takes at least three to six months for a model suited for fundamental investors to return to normal levels. If the under-estimation occurs in "normal" times, then there could be issues with the model specification.

Q: *Your model predicts the wrong market beta.*

A: There could be several reasons for this. First, the predicted beta might not be to your regional benchmark, but to a custom bench-mark based on the estimation universe of the risk model. Some-times this is not made sufficiently clear. My preference is to enable the PM with her favorite benchmark, provided that it satisfies a few requirements: it has to be sufficiently broad and representa-tive of the market; and it has to be sufficiently liquid, via an ETF or a future, or both. Secondly, the beta is estimated with respect to a risk model, which in turn may not be adequate for the purpose. For example, using a global model (i.e., representing all tradable world assets) to estimate the beta of a European portfolio to the STOXX50 is not advisable. Better choose a European model.

Q: *Your model predicts a beta that is different from the Bloomberg beta.*

A: The Bloomberg beta (*BETA* ⟨*GO*⟩) is a historical beta. It is esti-mated by performing a linear univariate regression of an asset's returns against the benchmark returns. All the observations are equal weighted. The model beta is estimated based on the model's factor covariance matrix and is a *predicted beta*. The factor covari-ance matrix and the idiosyncratic volatilities are estimated using more sophisticated methods than equal weighting. The historical beta is a less accurate measure of forward-looking sensitivity for

several reasons. First, while the risk model is also based on historical data, it weights past observations using a weighting scheme
that discounts observations further in the past, and is optimal for
the forecast horizon of interest (e.g.) two months out. Historical
betas are equal-weighted, with no horizon optimization. Second,
both factor and idio volatilities are estimated separately, with different weighting schemes. Third, modelers apply several advanced
adjustments for the estimates that capture time-series dependen-
cies and changes in volatility regimes. Taken together, these methods make a difference.

Q: *In Section 3.4.2 (Table 3.6) you say that the idiosyncratic volatility
of the benchmark is essentially zero. But why?*

A: Let us consider the easy part first: the beta of the benchmark is by
definition, one, because the beta is computed with respect to the
benchmark itself. Now, for the idiosyncratic volatility. The sum of
the weights of the constituents is one. By Pythagoras's Theorem
(again, in Section 3.4.2), the squared volatility of the portfolio is
the sum of the squared volatilities of its constituents:

$$(weight\ stock\ 1)^2 \times (idio\ vol\ stock\ 1)^2 + ...$$
$$+ (weight\ stock\ n)^2 \times (idio\ vol\ stock\ n)^2$$

Now, take the largest idiosyncratic volatility among the constituents, and denote it σ_{max}. The sum above is smaller than

$$[(weight\ stock\ 1)^2 + ... + (weight\ stock\ n)^2]\sigma_{max}^2$$

If sum of the weights is one, then the sum of the squared weights
is much smaller than one. For example, if the weights are all equal
to $1/n$, then the idiosyncratic variance is equal to $(1/n^2 + ... + 1/n^2)\sigma_{max}^2 = \sigma_{max}^2/n$. The idiosyncratic volatility is $\sigma_{max}/\sqrt{n}$. Since
n is usually at least equal to 50, and can be as large as several
thousands, then the idiosyncratic vol is small. In practice, on one
side the weights are not all identical, and this makes diversification
worse; but on the other, stocks with the largest weights are the
large-cap companies, with lower idiosyncratic risk, and therefore
their contribution to the sum is damped.

Q: *I know linear algebra and statistics and want to learn more about the
details of the estimation process. Can you recommend a reference?*

A: The short survey paper [Connor and Korajczyk, 2010] (also available online) is a good starting point. The book by the same authors et al. [Connor et al., 2010] is suitable for self-study and as a reference. The collections [Jurczenco, 2015; Litterman, 2003] are also useful.

4.3   ★The Machinery of Risk Models

As we mentioned, the distinctive feature of characteristic models is that they use stock features (or characteristics) as primitives. Characteristics are numerical values: each stock, at each date, and for each characteristic type (the "factor"), has one specific value. For each date, each factor has an associated return. For example, consider the market beta of a stock as its characteristic. The associated factor is the "market", proxied by a weighted portfolio of the traded stocks; and the market return is just the return of that portfolio. For the size factor, the characteristic is the order of magnitude of the market capitalization (e.g., the logarithm of the market cap) of a stock, and so on. Characteristics are intuitive, factor models less so. The goal of this section is to give an intuitive explanation of how factor models are constructed and estimated.

Perhaps the easiest way to think about a factor model is as a *superposition* of effects on the stocks. A wave breaking on the shore does not have a perfect, sinusoidal shape. It is made of a large wave, and then of a few smaller waves riding on it, and then many ripples on top of the smaller waves. These effects *sum up*. Similarly, stock returns are the effect of a large shock (the market), then a few smaller ones (sectors, the larger style factors), then a few even smaller ones. And then there are shocks that are specific to each stock only and that need to be estimated separately. Like waves, many of these movements have similar amplitude over time. In technical terms, we say that their volatility is persistent. This is a blessing, because it allows us to estimate future volatilities from past ones. In some cases, however, the volatility of a factor is not very persistent: in the case of the short interest, hedge fund holdings or of momentum, the factors experience large returns; you can think of these large returns as the tsunami that will wreak havoc on your portfolio if you are not prepared for it. We will cover them in detail in the next chapter.

There are many steps in the generation of a fundamental risk model. The major tasks involved are:

1. On each date, in advance of market open, an up-to-date list of characteristics of the stocks are received from data vendors, checked for data integrity, and preprocessed; for example, certain loadings are scaled and centered, so that average of the loadings over a certain investment universe is zero, and their standard deviation is one. These characteristics are arranged into a *loadings matrix* **B** with a number of rows equal to the number of assets, and a number of columns equal to the number of characteristics.

2. Factor returns and idiosyncratic returns for the previous day are estimated using a cross-sectional linear regression. This means that the stock returns are the dependent variable (the "y" in a regression equation) and the matrix of stock characteristics are the independent variables. The estimates – the regression coefficients – are the factor returns; the list of factor returns is more or less universally denoted by **f**. The residuals of the regression are the idiosyncratic returns (or residual returns) of the stock; and the vector of residuals, like the symbol for residuals in undergraduate statistics courses, is denoted by the symbol ϵ.

3. Once the latest factor and idiosyncratic returns are estimated, we enrich the existing time series of these returns and, using the entire time series, estimate the factor covariance matrix and the individual idiosyncratic volatilities.

As a byproduct of the second step, the estimation procedure also generates portfolios, one for each factor. These portfolios have returns equal to the factor returns; hence the term *factor-mimicking portfolios* (FMPs). They play an important role for performance attribution and hedging. The process is exemplified in Figure 4.2. These steps are repeated every day.

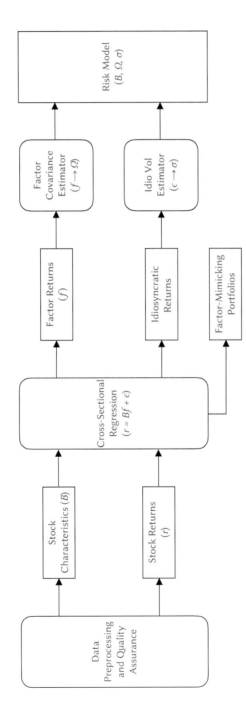

Figure 4.2 Steps needed to generate a risk model.

42

4.4   Takeaway Messages

There are three types of factor models:

1. *Fundamental;*
2. *Time series;*
3. *Statistical.*

Fundamental models rely on characteristics of the individual stocks and are commonly used by fundamental investors. They describe two features of returns:

1. Their *expected returns;*
2. Their *risk.*

Chapter 5

Understand Factors

- *What will you learn here:* The definition and interpretation of the most important risk model factors, with a special emphasis on style factors.
- *Why does this matter:* If a factor model is the skeleton of the market, then the factors are the large muscles of the body. They literally move the markets. You may want to give them a name, and know how they do it.
- *When will you need this:* You will revisit this chapter during large drawdowns, looking for clues; and on a periodic basis, when you want to parse sell-side reports discussing factor "rotations".

F actors partially explain stock returns. They exhibit trends (i.e., non-zero expected returns) and volatilities. Many of these factors were first introduced to describe puzzling returns not explained by the CAPM. Researchers provide two explanations for the existence of a non-null factor return. First, these returns could be the compensation a portfolio manager receives for the risk taken in the portfolio. Investors are rational after all, and don't leave money on the table, in the form of non-priced risk. However, some researchers push for "behavioral" explanations, in which the expected returns stem from investors' bounded rationality: investors have cognitive biases, inability to process infinite information and to perform complex optimizations in their head. I am presenting both, because, while the former seems more relevant to risk management, the latter helps the investor interpret the factor.

Like rabbits, factors come in many guises; like rabbits, they multiply at an exponential rate. Commercial vendors err on the side of safety and include a large number of factors in their models (usually between 50 and 100). Figure 5.1 shows the correlation matrix of a popular model. There are several clusters of highly correlated factors on the diagonal: there is a financials cluster, a health-care cluster, a consumer retail cluster, and several others industry clusters. The highest correlation cluster is made of the factors related to the broad market: "market", "market sensitivity", and "volatility". In addition, there are groups of correlations that have an intuitive interpretation.

- Group #1 shows that there are positive correlations between two groups of production inputs: "metals and mining", "chemicals", "construction materials" on one side, and "paper and forest products" to "construction engineering".
- Group #2 shows that these same industrial outputs are positively correlated with market factors, i.e., these industries are cyclical.
- Group #3 shows that financial industries are also cyclical.
- Group #4 shows a positive correlation between cyclical industries that are connected via supply chain relationship (products, and their retail channels): "consumer durables", "autos" and "auto parts" on one side, "multiline retail", "distributors", "luxury goods" on the other.

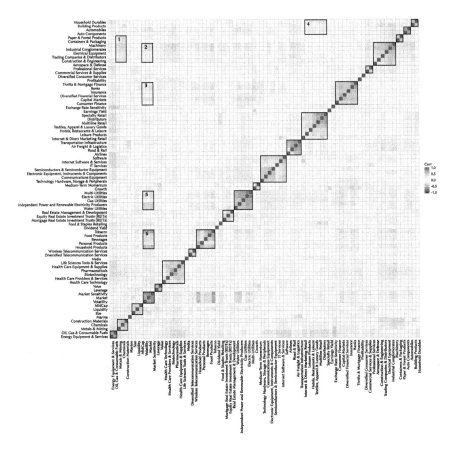

Figure 5.1 Summary correlation matrix between the factor returns of a US model (Axioma AXUS4) for the years 2008–2017.

- Groups #5 and #6 show that utilities and consumer staples industries are negatively correlated with the market factors returns, consistently with their status as defensives.

The factors in the first four groups are termed *style factors*, and their description takes most of this chapter. For the sake of brevity, I describe those factors that seem material, experimentally robust, investable, and interpretable. I classify them in four sets:

1. **The economic environment**: country, beta, industries, volatility.
2. **The trading environment**: short interest, active manager holdings.

3. **Technical Factors**: momentum continuation and reversal.
4. **The company's valuation**: value, profitability, growth.

5.1 The Economic Environment

A handful of factors show high return correlations to each other. Although they have different interpretations and behaviors, we consider them together.

5.1.1 Country

The first factor is the simplest: the *country* factor, sometimes also termed the market factor (Figure 5.2). Each stock has unit exposure to this factor. This is the Great Equalizer: when it moves, all stocks are affected the same way. This also means that a portfolio that is neutral the country factor is effectively dollar-neutral, because the total exposure is equal to zero:

$$0 = 1 \times NMV_1 + \ldots 1 \times NMV_n = NMV_1 + \ldots NMV_n$$

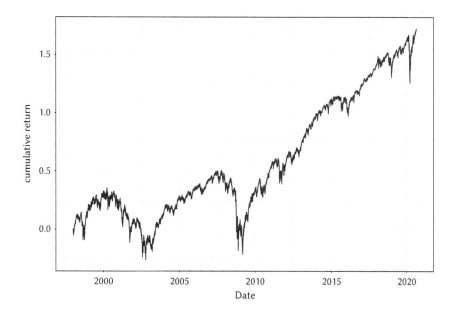

Figure 5.2 Time Series of the country factor cumulative returns, 2007–2017.

Vendors also offer multi-country models, which cover regions (Europe, Asia Pacific, North America); in these models there is not a single country factor, but many; typically one per country, although it is conceivable that two different countries may have the same country factor because of very similar economic exposures.

Interpretation. You can interpret it as a baseline factor, whose returns are close to the average of the returns of the stocks traded. It is called a country factor because, when the risk model includes assets from different countries, it usually describes the country risk of a stock by giving it a unit exposure to the country to which it belongs. Its expected returns are positive because, to a first approximation, on any given day they are the average of the asset returns on that same day, and this equal-weighted average return is positive.

5.1.2 Industries

Industry factors are a natural extension of countries. In a global risk model, countries are a partition of the global investment universe. In a country risk model, industries are a partition of a country's investment universe. Like in the case of countries, there is one factor per industry, and a stock has unit exposure to that industry if it satisfies some criterion for inclusion; otherwise it has zero exposure. Sometimes the criterion adopted is an official classification scheme. A popular such scheme is the Global Industry Classification Standard (GICS), developed and maintained by MSCI and Standard & Poor's. GICS has four levels, ranging from sectors to sub-industries. In other cases, risk model providers create a custom classification, which is more tailored to the risk model's intended use. Most notably, the investment universe in some countries does not contain all the GICS industries, and this requires some pruning and aggregation of the original classification. Table 5.1 shows how loadings look for a sample of companies in the US and Canada across a handful of sectors. Factor models usually go one level deeper, to the industry level.

Interpretation. The interpretation of an industry factor's return is different from the return of a simple capitalization-weighted portfolio of stocks in that industry, as in the case of sector SPDRS. The interpretation of the risk model's industry portfolio is more involved. It has

Table 5.1 Country and industry loadings for a sample of US and Canadian companies.

Ticker	USA	Canada	Ind.	Fin.	Tech.	Cons.
AAPL	1	0	0	0	1	0
ATD	0	1	0	1	0	1
BBD	1	0	1	0	0	0
F	0	1	1	0	0	0
GE	1	0	1	0	0	0
GOOG	1	0	0	0	1	0
GS	1	0	0	1	0	0
L	0	1	0	1	0	1
MGI	0	1	0	0	1	0
MS	1	0	0	1	0	0
MSFT	1	0	0	0	1	0
RCI	0	1	0	0	1	0
RY	0	1	0	1	0	0
SJR	0	1	0	0	1	0
T	1	0	0	0	1	0
TD	0	1	0	1	0	0
TSLA	1	0	1	0	0	0
WMT	0	1	0	1	0	1

unit exposure to that industry and no exposure to any other industries, like an industry benchmark. In addition, it has no exposure to any style factor. Whereas the Technology SPDR ETF may have, at some point in time, a positive momentum exposure because all its members have enjoyed positive returns, an industry media factor portfolio will have no momentum exposure. The benefit of the factor-based approach is that its returns are not conflating the returns of several factors: you know that internet media has positive returns not because of its momentum content. In addition, a factor exists for each industry, rather than at the more aggregated sector level, as is the case for many popular benchmarks. If you inspect the industry portfolios estimated with a factor model, you will notice that they contain a large number of stocks, usually ranging in the thousands. The reason is that, even if the industry contains only a few hundred stocks, the industry portfolio employs additional stocks in order to eliminate the exposure to all factors that are not the industry itself.

Insight 5.1 Industry Factors and sector ETFs.

Industry Factors have different returns than sector ETFs. They are more granular and have no exposure to style factors.

5.1.3 Beta

The second factor is the *beta* (or *market sensitivity*) factor. We have encountered this factor in the first chapter. The beta exposure of a stock is its historical sensitivity to the "market" returns; in the US it is common to use the returns of the S&P 500. I put *market* in quotes because the definition of the market is slightly arbitrary[1] [Roll, 1977]. Should it be all equity assets in the US? All equity assets in the world? All tradable assets to investors? The choice of the S&P 500 is motivated by a few considerations. First, all investors are familiar with it; second, it is sufficiently broad and representative of the US "investable" universe (i.e., sufficiently liquid), so that the choice of a broader index (say, the Russell 3000) does not result in very different betas.

A few words on the way this factor is estimated, in case you want to reproduce it on your own, or want to compare it to other betas (say, the Bloomberg-generated beta). In commercial risk models, the time series regression does not give equal importance to all past daily returns. Recent days are weighted more than days far in the past, usually exponentially so: for example, yesterday is fully weighted at 1, the day before is weighted at 1/2, the next day at 1/4, and so on; in practice the weighting scheme is such that the historical horizon used in the regression ranges between four and twelve months.[2] Moreover, the weighting scheme could be even slightly more sophisticated than the exponential one.

---

[1] One of the early and influential criticisms of the CAPM was in fact that we don't know and can't know the market portfolio.

[2] More precisely, this means that the weighted sum of observation ages is, for example, four months:

$$w \times 1 + w^2 \times 2 + w^3 \times 3 + \ldots + w^t \times t + \ldots = 80 \text{ trading days}$$

In this case, the weight for day t would be $w^t = (80/81)^t$.

Interpretation. Consider a dollar-neutral portfolio that is long high-beta assets and short low-beta assets.[3] You would expect the portfolio to have positive returns because, according to the Capital Asset Pricing Model, high-beta assets have greater sensitivity to the market, and the market has positive expected returns. This is however not the case. In fact, taking the *opposite* view – shorting high-beta names and going long low-beta names – yields positive returns. This strategy is often termed "betting against beta (BAB)", after an influential paper [Frazzini and Pedersen, 2014] on the subject. This result is robust and is very relevant to the fundamental investors for two reasons. The first one is related to performance. If the investor's portfolio is long the beta factor, then the performance will suffer somewhat from this exposure, since the factor's expected returns are negative. We want to measure the impact of this exposure and, at the very least, weight if the size of the negative PnL attribution is too high compared to the idiosyncratic PnL of the portfolio. If it is, then setting an upper limit on the beta exposure makes sense.

Understanding performance matters; understanding the risk associated to this factor is no less important, and the two are naturally related. Why does this factor lose money? How fast? And in what investing environment can we expect to see the factor lose money? As is often the case, there is no agreement on the causes of the anomaly. Frazzini and Pedersen (F&P henceforth) note that many investors face constraints when investing. Some institutional investors, for example, are not allowed to short stocks and to apply leverage to their portfolio. F&P suggest that these investors will seek higher returns by holding stocks with higher sensitivity to the market; higher beta should after all imply higher returns. By doing so, they provide excess demand for these stocks, which increase in price. Eventually the intrinsic value of the stock dominates, and the subsequent returns are negative. In this interpretation, the beta factor returns will be positive when we are in a "risk-on" environment (Figure 5.3). Investors are bullish, their risk appetite grows, and the way this is expressed in a portfolio is by buying riskier stocks linked to the economic trends. The opposite happens in a "risk-off" environment. In addition, in a sell-off environment, all stocks become more

---

[3] More details about the exact weights are given in Section 4.3.

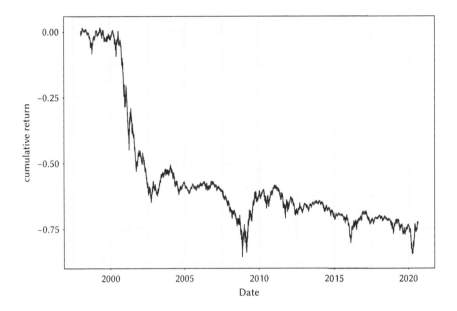

Figure 5.3   Time Series of the Beta factor cumulative returns, 1998–2020.

correlated to each other and to the market. It is often said that "in a crisis, all correlations go to one". A similar phenomenon occurs with betas. For example, in Figure 5.4 I take the Russell 3000 constituents, estimate their historical betas on each date and display, for every date, the difference between the 75th percentile of the betas and the 25th percentile on that date (the interquantile range). The range of variation decreases rapidly between Sept. 1, 2008 and January 1, 2009, i.e., in the most acute period of the 2008 financial crisis. This phenomenon is termed *beta compression* and is documented by Frazzini and Pedersen. The implication for a fundamental investor is that he or she can interpret its returns as a barometer of the overall risk appetite in the market, and that high exposures can be especially risky in a sudden derisking regime change.

Another potential explanation has to do with the relationship between this factor and the next one on our list: the volatility factor, which we analyze next.

In the discussion above, we have always assumed that the loading in the risk model is the "raw" loading, typically a number greater than zero and usually close to one. You may want to keep in mind that this

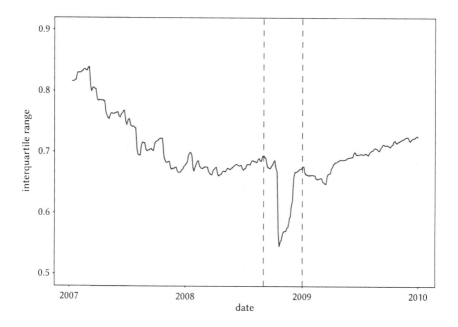

Figure 5.4 Beta compression phenomenon.

loading is sometimes transformed by *z-scoring* it. Z-scoring is a simple operation, which consists first of subtracting from all the loadings the average loading of all assets and then dividing the resulting number by the standard deviation of the loadings:

(z-scored loading of an asset)

$$= \frac{(raw \ loading \ of \ an \ asset) - (average \ of \ all \ loadings)}{(standard \ deviation \ of \ all \ loadings)}$$

The first step *centers* the betas. Whereas the raw beta of the benchmark was one, its z-scored beta is now equal to zero. The second step *scales* the beta using a natural unit of measure: the standard deviation. If betas are approximately normally distributed, this helps tell you how big is the beta of an asset compared to the other assets in the investment universe. If an asset has a z-scored beta equal to one, then the asset is in the top 16% high-beta assets; if the z-scored beta is two, then it is in the top 2%, and only 0.13% of assets should have a beta of 3 or greater.

5.1.4   *Volatility*

The volatility factor is easy to describe broadly: its returns are those of a portfolio that is long high-volatility stocks and short low-volatility stocks (Figure 5.5). Go down one level, and there are plenty of details: which volatility, total return volatility or idiosyncratic volatility? And over what time interval do we estimate the volatility? The behavior of the factor is robust to definitions, and can be summarized as: *the volatility factor has negative returns.* There is a direct relationship to the beta factor, because the beta depends on the stock volatility. From univariate regression, we know that the beta of a stock to the market is given by the formula

$$beta = (correlation\ of\ stock\ to\ market) \times \frac{(stock\ volatility)}{(market\ volatility)}$$

Market volatility identically affects all stock. If all stocks have the same correlation to the market, then beta and volatility would be just proportional to each other. Correlations are not identical across stocks. Whether this is sufficient to make the beta factor a distinct one from

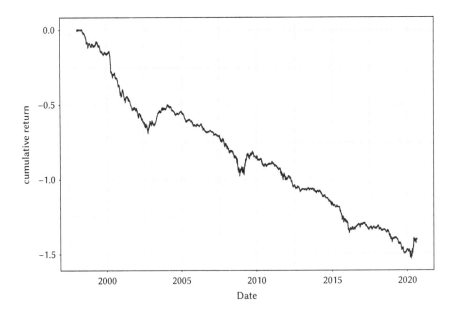

Figure 5.5   Time Series of the Volatility factor cumulative returns, 2007–2017.

the volatility one is still not settled. Many of the considerations we make for the volatility factor hold for beta, too.

Interpretation. The factor has received more attention than many other factors because it has survived the test of time and is quite strong: investing in low-volatility stocks and shorting high-volatility stocks, while being neutral to most other factors, yields large risk-adjusted performance. A large number of papers attempt to explain the low-volatility anomaly in two ways:

- The volatility anomaly follows from investors' preferences and constraints; this is the approach followed by F&P. Other mechanisms can explain why volatile stocks are overpriced. [Blitz et al., 2014] note that the original CAPM makes other assumptions which are violated beyond frictionless, unconstrained investing. For example, portfolio managers often care about relative performance; they are envious rather than greedy. In addition, their incentive resembles a call option: a floor in the case of a poor performance, and no ceiling in the case of a good one. All these considerations can inflate the demand for volatile stocks.
- Once we include other stock characteristics, the anomaly disappears. After adding profitability (e.g., Earnings-to-Price) and value (Book-to-Price) as characteristics (see below) in the model, the excess returns of low-vol stocks (and beta) disappear (see, for example, [Beveratos et al., 2014; Fama and French, 2016; Novy-Marx, 2016]).

How is this relevant to the fundamental investor? There are a few takeaways. First, the characteristics of beta, volatility, and profitability[4] overlap to a large degree, and describe broadly a company with "bond-like" characteristics, generating dividends to investors, exhibiting less volatility than its peers. It is useful to see what is the exposure to this overall theme in your portfolio. It enriches and quantifies other types of exposures monitored by investors, like the cyclical-vs-defensive balance in a portfolio, which usually is described in bespoke ways that depend on the industries covered by the investor.

---

[4] N.B.: a highly profitable stock is typically a low-volatility and low-beta one. So, whereas the beta and vol factors have negative expected returns, the profitability factor has a positive one.

Secondly, these factors do have a non-zero risk-adjusted return. By having positive exposure to beta and volatility, the portfolio manager incurs expected losses. These losses usually are justified by the fact that among stocks with high volatility there are some that exhibit strong idiosyncratic performance. The good portfolio manager has an edge in identifying them. However, it is important to quantify the incurred cost.

5.2   The Trading Environment

According to a risk model, asset returns are driven by factor returns. But what drives factor returns? To a first approximation, we consider factors as random and independent from the past. Certainly, there is short-term dependence in returns; but it dissipates after one or two days, and cannot be exploited by fundamental investors. We model the market as the aggregation of preferences of many small investors, none of whom are able to influence its returns. The everyday experience of a portfolio manager is very different. Not only are asset returns driven by factors external to the investment universe, but also the behavior of investors reacting to asset returns affects factors in a continuous feedback loop. The relevant characteristic of an asset is its *ownership level* among active investors. This can be partially identified both on the short and on the long sides by means of different data sources.

5.2.1   Short Interest

If an investor has a negative outlook on an asset, she can short it, i.e., borrow the stock, sell it, then purchase it at a later date and return it to the owner (Figure 5.6). The process of borrowing is costly. A net *borrow rate* (or *borrow fee*) is charged to the trader [Fabozzi, 2004]. There are several available shorting metrics, among them:

- *Short Ratio:* Short Interest divided by the market capitalization of the company;
- *Short-to-Float:* Short Interest divided by the market value of traded stocks;

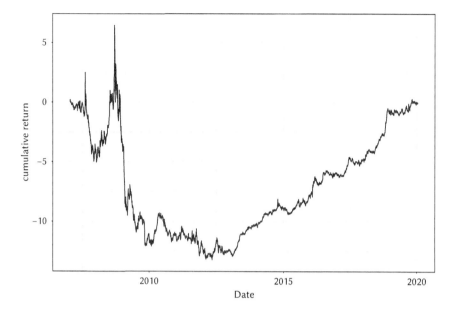

Figure 5.6   Time Series of the Short Interest factor cumulative returns, 2007–2017.

- *Days-to-Cover:* Short Interest divided by the average trading volume of the underlying security;
- *Utilization Rate:* Short Interest divided by market value of stocks made available to loan by brokers;
- *Borrow Rate:* Average rate charged by brokers to short the stock.

The performance of these metrics as a risk factor varies slightly and depends heavily on the other factors included in the model.

Interpretation. Shorting a stock is risky. A stock can have returns greater than 100%, but cannot lose more than 100%. Investors who short stocks have two special features. First, they are more sophisticated than the population average; second, they are unconstrained, relative to a large fraction of the investing population, which has no-shorting constraints. These constraints reduce the natural demand for shorts, and as a result they cause a mispricing for these assets. The fact that a stock is heavily shorted indicates that informed investors believe that the stock is overpriced. As a stock characteristic, shorting can be included in a factor model and tested. The short interest usually denotes the market value of the stock lent by brokers at a given point in time. This is available either via regulatory reports (e.g., bimonthly NYSE reporting in the US), or via data providers, which query the brokers and aggregate them.

It is more important to understand why short interest has such a strong negative performance. This fact, which is now the consensus view, is not so obvious; as late as 1995 some of the conventional wisdom was that hight short interest predicted high future returns [Epstein, 1995]. There are several explanations. We mentioned the first one: institutional constraints introduce price distortions. The implication of this explanation is that, if active institutional managers with no-short constraints become smaller participants, the size of the anomaly should become smaller as well. Another possible explanation is that shorting is indicative of *dispersion belief* among investors in the valuation of a company. This is connected to the dispersion anomaly: a lack of consensus among sell-side analyst recommendations is related to poor future returns [Diether et al., 2002]. A third explanation is that informed investors correct short-term (past 5-day returns) overreaction [Diether et al., 2009]; in this respect, short interest is related to short-term reversal. Finally, an explanation of the short-interest anomaly is that it is a compensation for risk. The returns of a short position are left-skewed, which makes them inherently riskier. In addition, the returns of shorts can be affected by a self-reinforcing behavior of the investors, who cover the stock in times of distress, thus generating even higher return for the stock, not unlike running for the exit at the same time in a crowded theater. These phenomena do exist but are still not well understood empirically.

5.2.2   *Active Manager Holdings (AMH)*

We saw that short interest data describes the aggregate short positions of informed investors. Is it possible to obtain similar data for the long positions? The 1934 Securities Exchange Act (also known as the "'34 Act") was amended in 1975. The newly added Section 13(f) required institutional asset managers holding a portfolio with a fair market value exceeding $100M to report their long holdings on a quarterly basis [SEC, 1934]. The holdings are reported up to 45 days after the end of the quarter. Since then, the percentage of investors with portfolios exceeding the minimal threshold has increased, and 13(f) data has become an indispensable source of information. Because of the regulatory disclosure requirements, the data have different features compared to short interest. First, they are far less current than short interest data, since the positions can be as old as 135 days. This drawback can be partially remedied by resorting to commercial data sets. The sellers of these data source and aggregate them from commercial entities, like prime brokerages. The reporting delays are shorter and the coverage goes beyond the United States. Secondly, 13(f) data are more disaggregated than short interest. We have the ability to analyze the holdings by investor Assets under Management, and most importantly investment style. The holdings of a purely quantitative, high-turnover investor are less informative than those of a long-biased, low-turnover, "tiger cub" (the hedge funds started by the alumni of J. Robertson's Tiger Management), which in turn are differently informative than those of an activist investor with extremely low turnover and a very concentrated portfolio. Therefore, there is not a single characteristic that can be extracted from this data, but rather many variants. This makes 13(f) data a very useful dataset.

Interpretation. AMH gives the investor some visibility into the investment choices of her peers. There is variation across investors, but there is commonality as well, and it is captured by the factor. If you think of the extreme case in which every hedge fund holds a copy of the same portfolio, then this factor is a measure of "crowding". In the absence of external shocks, the process is beneficial to consensus stocks, as different portfolio managers bid up the same stocks. However, if an adverse external event occurs that generates a sufficiently high loss for the aggregate portfolio (think a macroeconomic event like a recession forecast, or a catastrophe like Fukushima's disaster), then its holders react by "deleveraging" (or "derisking") their portfolio: they trade against their own positions. Since they all hold a similar portfolio, there is a temporary excess supply for their securities. This in turn generates further negative returns for their positions, which forces them to deleverage even more (see Figure 5.7). In this respect, even if the shock is exogenous, the risk is endogenous, in the sense that losses are amplified by the behavior of the actors, not by changes in asset valuations. The cycle comes to an end when their leverage ratio is at tolerable levels. Even though the cycle is initiated by an

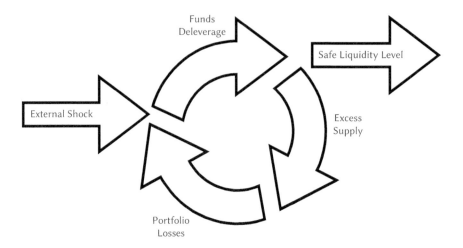

Figure 5.7   The deleveraging cycle.

external event that serves as catalyst, the deleveraging phenomenon is endogenous. Both the AMH factor and the short interest factor are proxy measures for the deleveraging process.

In Figure 5.8, we show the factor returns of a "vanilla" factor that only takes into account the holdings of fundamental long-short and long-biased hedge funds; for long biased, we process the data so as to estimate the "active" holding in excess of the benchmark, a standard procedure [Cohen et al., 2010; Angelini et al., 2019]. The performance of the factor was excellent in 2008, when, in the words of a consumer portfolio manager, picking up winners and losers was "like shooting fish in a barrel". The performance afterwards has been marginal, and has been characterized by rapid drawdowns at the end of 2015 and in 2016.

5.2.3   Momentum

The momentum characteristic of a stock is given by its past performance over a given interval compared to its peers (Figure 5.9). For example, one-month momentum is the return over the past month; 12-month is the return over the past year; and longer-term momentum factors are similarly defined. For the longest time traders have used recent and not-so-recent history in their investment decisions:

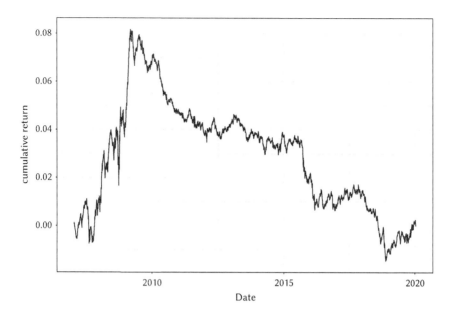

Figure 5.8 Time Series of the Active Manager Holdings factor cumulative returns, 2007–2017.

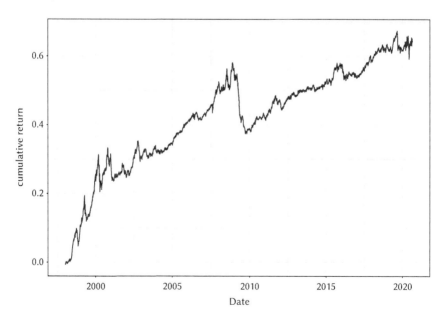

Figure 5.9 Time Series of the medium-term momentum factor cumulative returns, 1998–2020.

Table 5.2   Performance of stock and hypothetical portfolios, for
trend-following and momentum. Data are relative to Nov 28, 2019.

Stock	1-Yr Return (%)	TF Portfolio ($M)	MO Portfolio ($M)
FB	43.5	1	1
MSFT	40	1	1
GOOG	20.7	.5	0
IBM	11.2	0.25	0
NFLX	8.2	0.125	−1
AMZN	7.4	0.125	−1

for example, in Lefevre's classic [Lefèvre, 1923], the hero of the book
(legendary trader Jesse Livermore) uses a similar strategy in the
Boston boiler-rooms at the turn of the 20th century. Researchers
pointed out "inertia" in stock prices as early as 1937 [Cowles, 3rd and
Jones, 1937]; but the anomaly entered mainstream academic research
in the 1980s, with research by Jegadeesh and Titman [Jegadeesh
and Titman, 1993, 2011]. "Momentum" has a different meaning from
trend-following, because it is based on *relative* performance, whereas
the latter is based on absolute performance. As a toy example,
consider a small universe composed of technology stocks. None of
the stocks had negative trailing 12-month returns. Trend Following is
long in all the stocks, proportional to their returns. A simple Momentum strategy is long (equal weights) the top two stocks and short
the bottom stocks. Table 5.2 has the weights for the two portfolios. A
momentum-based portfolio generated by a risk model would be closer
to the MO portfolio above, with some twists described in Section 4.3.

Momentum is a robust anomaly. It has been observed in many
equity markets (US, Europe, Asia, with the notable exception of
Japan), in many asset classes [Asness et al., 2013] (equities, commodi-
ties, bonds) and over long time intervals [Geczy and Samonov, 2016]
(two centuries). The reason for its continued outperformance cannot
be ascribed to characteristics of stocks alone. For stocks, however,
momentum has a well-identified term structure [Novy-Marx, 2012]:

- Strong (weak) performance in the previous 0–1 months is reverting:
  winners (losers) in the past month are losers (winners) in the near
  future. The effect is stronger as the historical observations are shortened. Strong performance in the past week is reverting more than
  strong performance in the past month, for example.

- Performance in the interval between one month and one year shows continuation – i.e., true momentum.
- Performance beyond a year in the past is reverting. For example, a stock with large positive returns in the period between 15 months ago and a year ago will have negative expected returns, every other characteristic being equal.

In addition to the term structure, there is an industry structure, i.e., industry indices as a whole have momentum, and momentum within an industry has distinctive characteristics (it can be weaker or stronger).

Interpretation. The most frequently mentioned explanations are both investor overreaction *and* investor underreaction. Perhaps investors underreact to news because they are overconfident and inattentive, especially when the flow of information is continuous and not very salient, to the point where it gets ignored; investors are like "frogs in the pan", not realizing that the environment is changing under their feet and reacting with a delay [Da et al., 2014]. But then, of course, investors may overreact to returns and extrapolate them into the future, generating demand for the stock and thus feeding further optimism [Delong et al., 1990]. Even a cursory read of the research on momentum will convince you that *we don't understand the origins of momentum.* We have complex, hard-to-falsify theories based on observational data. If overreaction or underreaction are behind momentum, then why does momentum exhibit reverting behavior at short horizons, continuation behavior at medium horizons, and reversion behavior again at long horizons? In addition to behavioral explanation of momentum, the last decade has seen the emergence of risk-based explanations. The return of a momentum strategy is compensation for risk, and specifically for *tail risk*, i.e., the risk that a momentum portfolio will experience large losses. This is visible in Figure 5.10. In this picture, we first z-score the daily factor returns with the estimated volatility of the factor in the previous three months. This step is necessary to make returns across different periods and different volatilities comparable. Then, we compute the quantiles of these scaled momentum returns. For example, the 5% quantile is the threshold for which returns below this value occur in 5% of the days in the historical sample. If the 5% quantile is negative and even lower

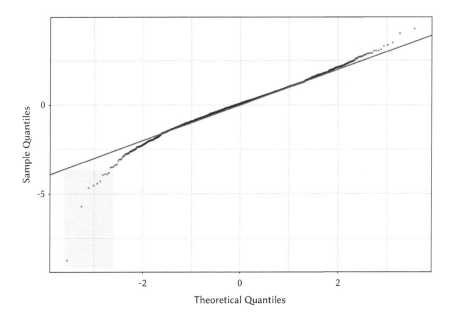

Figure 5.10 Quantile-Quantile plot of the medium-term momentum factor cumulative returns, 2007–2017. Factor returns are z-scored using rolling three-month realized volatility. The red rectangle highlights the heavy left tail of the return distribution.

than the quantile for the normal distribution, then this means that for the same probability value, larger negative returns will occur for the momentum distribution than for bell-distributed returns. Factor returns are heavier-tailed than the norm. Figure 5.10 confirms this phenomenon: we plot momentum quantiles on the y axis versus normal quantiles on the x axis. The left tail is below the red line, which corresponds to the case in which momentum is distributed like a Gaussian. These quantiles are very large, corresponding to large drawdowns. These results are confirmed and extended in an important paper by Daniel and Moskowitz [Daniel and Moskowitz, 2016]. This fact suggests that momentum returns are not earned for free. The price to pay is the risk of large, sudden losses. In this vein, two additional studies [Chabi-Yo et al., 2018; Ruenzi and Weigert, 2018] define a stock characteristic, the *Lower Tail Dependence* (or LTD), which describes the probability that the stock exhibits large losses when the market exhibits a large loss; think of it as a "left tail" beta. This is an intuitive and undesirable feature of a stock. Then, the authors show that viewing this characteristic as an additional factor makes momentum redundant, i.e., the LTD factor has positive returns (like momentum) and, given LTD, momentum's returns become insignificant. An additional feature of momentum losses is that the losses of the factor portfolio come from its short side, not the long one. The Great Recession case is instructive. During 2008, Momentum experienced higher volatility but did not lose money (see Figure 5.9). However, in 2009 the stocks that had experienced large losses in the previous year rallied as the market rebounded. These stocks had negative momentum, and were therefore held short in the momentum portfolio. To be sure, the long side of the momentum portfolio also appreciated, but not as much; hence the large loss of the momentum factor as a whole. If you look closely, in early 2016 momentum experienced another crash; this one concentrated among energy stocks like Chesapeake Energy Co. (CHK) and Seadrill Limited (SDRL), which had experienced steady losses since early 2014, and had a runup of 200–350% in the period February–March 2016. The reason behind the bullwhip return of the short side of momentum is not entirely clear. An intuitive explanation, which should resonate with the fundamental investor, is the following. According to the well-known Merton Model of corporate debt [Merton, 1974] you can view a stock as a call option on the assets of a company. The owner of the company can decide to shut down the company, liquidate the assets, pay back its debts, and receive the balance. The price of the company is the value of this option. When a company has large negative momentum loadings, the value of the option has decreased, and the company's assets have therefore lost value. If the option was in the money, now it's less so, and may in fact be an out-of-the-money option. Like an out-of-the money option, the company's stock price is more sensitive to shocks in the value of its assets, or in the price of its debt, compared to an in-the-money option. Suppose that there is a common driver of the asset value for a group of comparable companies. In the simplest case, this could be proxied by the market returns, but in more specific cases it could be, for example, the availability of debt refinancing options for the group of companies. Then, this driver will cause a much larger appreciation of the short side of the momentum portfolio compared to the long side.

While behavioral explanations may be somewhat enlightening to the fundamental investor, the risk associated to holding momentum is concrete and always present. Recent history is punctuated with sudden, violent drawdowns. A successful portfolio manager unavoidably holds a portfolio that is long momentum, even without actively trading exposure to this factor. Long successful stocks eventually have a positive momentum loading; the opposite is true for the shorts. In both cases, the dollar momentum exposure of the portfolio increases naturally. The manager has to balance the upside of these positions with the risk implied in the momentum exposure. The good news is that the risk model gives a first estimate of this risk.

5.3   The Company: Valuation Factors

Characteristics of intrinsic value of a firm are estimated, refined, compared by analysts on a daily basis, since the dawn of fundamental investing. Unsurprisingly, there are so many such characteristics that some risk model providers don't employ them as individual factors, but rather group some of them into composites that serve as factors. It is not possible to go in detail into each one of them for a few reasons. First of all, there just are too many of them. One risk provider uses six characteristics just to define one factor (earnings quality); and there are many other variants. Secondly, a smaller subset of factors exhibits the necessary features of simplicity (elementary ratios), credibility (with a large out-of-sample history), and relevance in the events of large drawdowns. Lastly, it is likely that this large set of factors is subject to the problem of overfitting.

5.3.1   *Value*

The characteristic most frequently used to measure the value of a company is the book-to-price (BTOP, or B/P) ratio, i.e., the book value of common equity divided by the market capitalization. When Fama and French introduced their influential three-factor model [Fama and French, 1993], one of the three factors was BTOP (the other two being market and size). Value can be defined using alternative characteristics that seem to describe the same returns, and that may be more appropriate for certain industries:

- *Sales-to-Price:* the most recent company sales divided by the market capitalization;
- *Cash-Flow-to-Price:* the most recent cash flow (usually, free cash flow) divided by the market capitalization;
- *Earnings-to-Price:* trailing 12-month earnings or forward 12-month earnings predicted by analysts, divided by market capitalization;
- *EBITDA-to-EV:* trailing 12-month earnings before interest, taxes, depreciation and amortization (EBITDA) to Enterprise Value (EV);
- *Dividend Yield:* trailing or forecasted dividend, divided by price;
- *(Revenues-Cost of Goods Sold)/Assets;*
- *Net Income/Equity.*

The first two are used by some of MSCI© Barra's models; the third and the fourth are studied by Lakonishok, Shleifer and Vishny [Lakonishok et al., 1994]. Finally, the last characteristic is often used as independent factor in commercial models (MSCI© Barra, Axioma©). These four characteristics differ from BTOP in that they are ratios of a flow quantity (dollars per year) to a stock quantity (market capitalization), whereas BTOP is a ratio of a stock quantity to a stock quantity. Fama and French have repeatedly expressed a preference for this metric because (a) they find in their 1992 paper that it has greater explanatory power than alternative ratio; (b) it is more stable over time, since book value depends on the sum of earnings, not on the last one. Earnings-to-price is naturally related to dividend yield, which is usually treated as a separate factor. This suggests that the separation between factors is somewhat arbitrary. We already saw how volatility and quality are related and are broadly considered defensive factors. The relationship among the above characteristics, and between them and dividend yield, is similarly nuanced. Since "value" means different things to different people, fundamental investors disagree with the definition of value in risk models. If it's just BTOP, then usually the ratio is not equally meaningful for industries (as in the case of banks). If it is a combination of many descriptors, then it is viewed as hopelessly opaque. However, this factor, in its many descriptors, does describe one of the most important dimensions of investing. Indeed, the value/glamour dichotomy is one of the few essential ones by which an analyst classifies her portfolio, together with a few others like cyclical/defensive, international/domestic, and trending/contrarian.

Figure 5.11 shows a quartet of value factors. Earnings Yield is the combination of three terms: Realized earnings to price; Forecasted earnings-to-price, calculated as the 12-month forward-looking earnings estimate, divided by the average total issuer market capitalization computed over the last 30 calendar days; 12-month forward-looking IBES© consensus earnings estimates. Profitability is the combination of return-on-equity, return-on-assets, cash-flow-to-assets, cash-flow-to-income, gross margin, and sales-to-assets descriptors. Value: ratio of common equity to average 30-day total issuer market capitalization. Dividend Yield: the sum of the dividends paid (excluding nonrecurring, special dividends) over the most recent year, divided by the average total issuer market capitalization computed over the last 30 calendar days.

Interpretation. There are many possible explanations of why and how value works. The empirical evidence supporting these theories is not conclusive. Even so, it is useful to review them. They are arrows in the investor's quiver.

- Value gives a measure of the time horizon of the portfolio, in the following sense. Value and growth together can be interpreted as a *duration* exposure in the portfolio. Growth stocks receive most of their value from cash flows far into the future, not unlike a long-term bond. Value stocks, conversely are more similar to companies under distress, with a shorter time horizon; their valuation is realized at a much shorter horizon. [Petkova, 2006] finds that shocks to the term spread (the difference between long-term and short-term bonds yields) is correlated to the returns of value stocks.
- It captures a specific risk profile of the portfolio. Value stocks are intrinsically riskier than growth stocks in that they are more likely to incur earnings and dividend shocks. The excess return of a value stock is then a compensation for risk [Chen and Zhang, 1988]. If we further sort distressed firms according to BTOP, then high BTOP

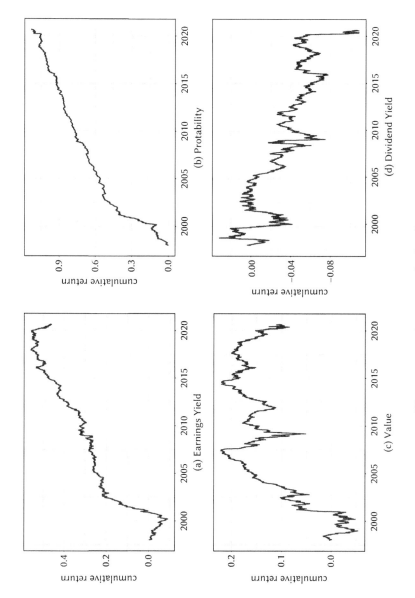

Figure 5.11 A quartet of value factors.

companies have higher returns than low-BTOP ones [Griffin and Lemmon, 2002].

- Moreover, this riskiness has an intuitive interpretation. Value stocks have high fixed costs and high levels of unproductive capital. The slack capacity generates downside risk during recessions, which is not matched by upside profitability in times of expansion. Pro-cyclical stocks must have a return premium, a fundamental and intuitive fact of asset pricing [Cochrane, 1999]. Value stocks are more sensitive to bad economic news (industrial production, inflation, money supply, interest rates); see [Black et al., 2009].

- Finally, the higher returns of value stocks may be due to investor behavior, and not to compensation for risk. If investors systematically overestimate growth of companies with high growth, for example, by extrapolating past growth, and underestimate the growth of low-growth companies, then companies with high growth (value) characteristics will experience a downward (upward) price correction. We expand on this explanation below.

A more quantitative approach to understanding the valuation anomaly is through Gordon's formula, which links the price of a security to its dividend, the dividend growth, and the required rate of return on the stock.

$$price = \frac{dividend}{(rate\ of\ return) - (growth\ rate)}$$

Alternatively, we replace dividend by the product of cash flow and payout ratio:

$$price = \frac{(payout\ ratio) \times (cash\ flow)}{(rate\ of\ return) - (growth\ rate)}$$

Rearrange the terms, so that we can link the cash-flow-to-price ratio to other fundamental quantities:

$$\frac{(cash\ flow)}{price} = \frac{(rate\ of\ return) - (growth\ rate)}{(payout\ ratio)}$$

Consider two stocks with different cash flow-to-price ratios. If their payout ratio is the same, the high valuation stock has then lower expected growth. A similar conclusion may be obtained with the earning-to-price (E/P) ratio. However, we can read Gordon's formula the other way around: if the forecasted growth of a company is revised upward, then its C/F ratio is depressed, and the stock becomes a "glamour" stock. The earnings growth is usually measured by past earnings growth, growth of sales (GS), 1-year or 2-year analyst consensus growth, or a weighted average of these. The behavioral interpretation of the value anomaly is that investors overshoot in their predictions. Specifically, Lakonishok, Shleifer and Vishny show that stocks with low past growth and low expected growth outperform their glamour counterparts (high past growth and high expected growth). After forming a portfolio long Value and short Glamour, the stocks do not show the same spread in growth as originally forecasted, and from this portfolio outperformance follows.

We have two takeaways from this overview of valuation factors. First: for the fundamental investor, valuation is an essential element of investing, and value factor exposures allow her to summarize an aggregate tilt of a portfolio at a glance. This is useful for portfolio *synthesis*. In the long run, these factors can explain a significant fraction of the PnL of a Portfolio manager. Secondly, as the chart of factor returns shows, the volatilities and the drawdowns and runups of these factors are not large. Understanding and managing the exposures to these factors matters for strategic positioning of a portfolio more than for short-run tactical portfolio management.

5.4   Takeaway Messages

Important factors that are common to many factor models are:

1. *Market: Country, Beta, Volatility.*
2. *Industries: Usually based on external classifications (GICS), occasionally a smaller custom set of factors.*
3. *Technical: Momentum and Reversal.*
4. *Valuation: Value and Growth.*
5. *Endogenous: Short Interest, Hedge Fund Holdings.*

Factors have *meanings*. They are in relationship with each other and with macroeconomic variables.

Chapter 6

Use Effective Heuristics for Alpha Sizing

- *What will you learn here:* How to transform single-stock investment theses into positions that result in the highest risk-adjusted performance. And how to set the size of your portfolio under changing market conditions.
- *Why do you need it:* Your goal is to be as profitable as possible while being resilient in any market condition. This chapter helps you be more profitable; the following ones help you become resilient.
- *When will you need this:* On a daily basis.

E d Thorp and Jim Simons are considered the most accomplished quantitative investors alive. Thorp has authored an autobiography, "A Man for all Markets", while Simons is the subject of the similarly titled biography "The Man Who Solved The Market".[1] These books don't reveal many details about the investment processes devised by these two managers, but you can read a message between the lines. "Alpha" – broadly defined as the buy and sell signals – was not sufficient to generate outsized returns, especially in equities. Renaissance Technology (Simon's firm) had identified alpha signals, but it took years until these would produce sizable revenues. It was only in the new millennium that its Sharpe Ratio went from an already-good 2 to an outstanding 6 and higher. What made this qualitative jump possible was *portfolio construction*. Portfolio construction is a process that takes many inputs and generates a single output. The inputs are stock expected returns, transaction costs, risk models, and a manager's risk tolerance and return objective. The output is a portfolio, updated on a weekly or daily basis; for some quantitative managers, it is updated every minute or even every second. To be effective, the process must be principled, rule-based, automated, and efficient. Portfolio construction is a competitive advantage for quantitative managers, if not *the* competitive advantage. Fundamental investors do not trade every second thousands of stocks; does it matter for them? The answer is yes, enormously. It is not sufficient to have great ideas. In order to extract the most from them in good times, and survive when they don't work as expected, a portfolio manager needs principles and rules. The good news is that these principles can be learned and adapted to a manager's style. Because a PM does not trade with the same frequency of a quantitative manager, automation and speed are not as important, even though they can help. This chapter focuses on the rules that a manager can follow with the support of some analytical tools that are widely available, but without the need of advanced tools like an optimizer or an automatic trading system. This simplicity has many virtues and very few drawbacks. At any time, you will completely understand the bets expressed in your portfolio.

---

[1] The love child of Simons and Thorp is clearly The Man Who Solved All the Markets (But Who Is Wealthy Enough Not to Care About It).

Consequently, if the portfolio doesn't perform as expected, it will be easy to identify what is not working as expected and correct the course. The daily job of a fundamental portfolio manager is a continuous learning process; the better the process, the faster the learning. Transparency also means that you will be able to act quickly, and with fewer chances to make mistakes. You may then ask, Why should I bother with portfolio optimization or other sophisticated techniques? Show me a few heuristics, and I will live happily ever after. This applies to 80%, maybe even 90% of portfolio managers. For these managers, heuristics without any optimization suffice, and are indeed the best option. Eventually, you may have to confront two big issues. The first one is efficiency: when returns become smaller because of increased market efficiency or higher costs, then even small gains matter, and a more systematic investment process will help achieve it. The second one is the cognitive cost of managing a portfolio. Your theses will become more sophisticated; your stock coverage broader; the risk requirement more stringent. All of this makes construction more time-consuming, which in turn takes time away from alpha research. These are nice problems to have, and are the subject of an optional section at the end of this chapter.

In order to invest effectively, you need three ingredients. First, you need an estimate of the expected returns of the stocks you cover. Secondly, you need to estimate the risk associated to a portfolio. Third, you need guidelines on your strategy's maximum risk. These guidelines are converted into constraints of the portfolio. The first two are the subject of this chapter. The last one is covered in Chapter 7.

6.1   Sharpe Ratio

This book uses return on GMV (usually shortened as "return") and Sharpe Ratio as the primary metric to evaluate performance. Returns play a major role in Chapter 9 on stop-loss decisions, and in Chapter 10 on leverage decisions. Sharpe Ratio and Information Ratio figure prominently in the other chapters. This section briefly defines the term and justifies its use. The *Sharpe Ratio* (SR) of the sequence of returns $r_1, r_2, \ldots$ is defined as the ratio of their average returns and their volatility:

$$Sharpe\ Ratio = \frac{(average\ return)}{(return\ volatility)}$$

The intuition for the Sharpe Ratio is that it provides a "risk-adjusted" measure of performance, compared to return. If volatility is a yardstick for risk, then the Sharpe Ratio is return measured in units of volatility. If you buy n units of volatility, the Sharpe Ratio tells you what payoff you receive.

There is a first wrinkle in the definition. In the academic financial literature, the Sharpe Ratio is defined on the returns in excess of the risk-free rate; this would be the rate of return of a riskless investment on the same horizon of the investment horizon of the strategy. As an important example, Gene Fama and Kenneth French evaluate Sharpe Ratio on portfolios rebalanced monthly, and use the 1-month T-bill as a risk-free rate. Practitioners, however, don't adjust for the risk-free rate: the sequence of returns they use in the calculation is the sequence of raw returns on GMV. There are several possible justifications for this choice if we really need one. Simplicity is one. Secondly, there is no intrinsic rebalancing horizon to a strategy, and for many fundamental portfolio managers, it is short enough that the risk-free rate adjustment does not make an actual difference; lastly, the existence of a risk-free asset is in itself dubious, which is a reason why academics themselves produce theories without the assumption that the risk-free asset exists. The *Information Ratio* (IR) is traditionally defined (see, e.g., [Grinold and Kahn, 1999]) in relationship to a benchmark's returns $r_1^b, r_2^b, \ldots$ Instead of the sequence of the raw strategy's returns, consider the sequence $r_1 - r_1^b, r_2 - r_2^b, \ldots$ Since many products try to outperform a benchmark, the Information Ratio gives a *relative* risk-adjusted measure of performance. As such, this definition will be used to communicate performance of index-related products to retail and institutional investors for the foreseeable future. However, practitioners use the term *Information Ratio* for the Sharpe Ratio computed on residual returns:

$$Sharpe\ Ratio = \frac{(average\ residual\ return)}{(residual\ return\ volatility)}$$

This is a natural extension of the common IR definition to the case when there is not a single factor (the benchmark) affecting returns, but many. There is no primacy among factors, and all of them should be subtracted from total returns. Under perfect hedging, the portfolio's returns will be the same as its idiosyncratic returns.

Why is Sharpe Ratio so ubiquitous and important? The intuition of the metric is clear. Return on GMV is performance relative to a *capital* budget. But the real scarce resource is not capital; it is risk. If your strategy has a high Sharpe Ratio, and low risk/GMV ratio, you can increase its leverage in order to bring its expected return to acceptable levels. Aside from fundamental investing, there are many relative-value strategies with high Sharpe and low risk/GMV ratio. In the absence of leverage (i.e., the ability to borrow additional capital against collateral at sufficiently low rates), these strategies would not be feasible; in the real world, they are implemented and often are extremely profitable. The whole of Chapter 10 is devoted to leverage.

Finally, you may object that the denominator of the Sharpe Ratio, i.e., volatility, is not the same as risk. Point taken; see Section 3.4.1. An entire book could be devoted to different measures of risk, e.g., [McNeil et al., 2005; Bacon, 2005]; and, to add insult to injury, the Sharpe Ratio itself has been heavily criticized: it does not distinguish between upside and downside risk, it is not consistent with logical preferences (in technical terms, it is not even a first-order stochastic dominant measure). Committees have been formed; replacements have been suggested, including the beautifully named "ulcer index" [Martin and McCann, 1989]; recommendations have been ignored. Titans of finance come and are quickly forgotten. Volatility and Sharpe will stay for the foreseeable future. Always think of volatility as an informative proxy of risk and imperfectly measured, and of the Sharpe Ratio as an imperfect, imperfectly measured, but useful, performance metric.

6.2   Estimating Expected Returns

The first step in portfolio construction, and perhaps the most important, is the conversion of fundamental convictions into dollar positions. This process is highly investor-specific, and may be based on methods that depend on the industry or the company. Relevant factors in the decisions may be:

- Output of cost and revenues based on detailed company-specific models;
- Macroeconomic projections;
- Investor sentiment and possible macroeconomic risks;
- Insights from meetings with the company's management;
- Long-term insights on changes in industry structure.

What is relevant here is that the returns be expressed as (a) idiosyncratic returns; (b) in expectation; and (c) over a common investment horizon for all the stocks under coverage. We go over each one of them.

Insight 6.1 Thinking about expected returns.

When you reason about stock returns, separate idiosyncratic returns from factor returns. What matters are the returns relative to the market and the industry of a stock.

First, views should be primarily based on idiosyncratic returns. By this I mean that the investor should consider carefully whether the investment in a stock is implicitly an industry bet, a country bet, or a style bet (e.g., investing in a high-growth stock). How can you think about this? Say that a certain company has a current price of $53 and that you have a price forecast of $74 at six months, a return of %40. The first question is whether you have a forecast on the returns of the stock's industry. If you average your forecasts on the stocks that you cover and are in the industry, you may have a rough estimate of your bullishness on the industry itself; alternatively, you may develop independently a view on the industry's expected returns six-months out; say this forecast is 15%; then your expected return on the stock is %25, not %40. To be sure: it is not wrong to invest in stocks with style and industry risk. The factor-based analysis of the portfolio will reveal these implicit bets and control their risk, which is one benefit of using factor risk models. However, in the stock selection process and before the portfolio construction one, it is still useful to ask which is the true source of alpha. What matters is the return of a stock relative to its industry and to the market. In a balanced portfolio, i.e., one with small risk coming from systematic sources, the country/industry/style PnL of one stock will be counterbalanced by opposite PnL in other stocks. Factor sources of returns are a nuisance rather than a true source of alpha.

Secondly, the returns should be in expectation. Investors usually formulate scenarios, and assign to each of them subjective probabilities. Under each scenario, they estimate the return of the stock. The input to the portfolio construction should be the expected return, i.e., the sum-product of returns and probabilities.

Thirdly, the expected returns should be expressed over the same investment horizon. If stocks have different horizons, they should be made consistent by scaling them to a common one. Say that we set the horizon at three months; then we multiply the expected return by the ratio (3 months)/(stock's investment horizon). The three-month horizon is arbitrary. What matters is that, whenever forecasts for different stocks are at different horizons, they should be adjusted so that longer-horizon forecasts get adjusted downward compared to short-horizon ones (Procedure Box 6.1).

Procedure 6.1 Estimate expected returns.

For each stock in your universe:

1. Set an investment horizon T, and a price forecast at that horizon.
2. Compute the forecasted total return at that horizon $r_{total} =$ (*price forecast*)/(*current price*) $- 1$.
3. Estimate industry returns $r_{industry}$ over the same horizon.
4. Estimate *forecasted idiosyncratic* return $r_{idio} = r_{total} - r_{industry}$.

Convert all the expected returns to the same investment horizon by dividing the return by the horizon: $\alpha = \bar{r}/T$.

6.3   Risk-Based Sizing

How do we convert these ideas into action? There are complicating factors:

- What about the risk of the stock's returns? For example, say that stock A has in your view an expected return of 15% in one-year horizon while stock B has only 10%. However, the annualized volatility of stock A is 30% while stock B's is 15%. How would this piece of information enter into your sizing decisions?
- Stocks are part of a portfolio; usually a new investment idea is added to a portfolio. How does the existing portfolio affect your sizing decision?
- Your knowledge of returns is imprecise. You may think that stock A is a better opportunity than stock B; but when you analyze your past decisions, you learn that your relative value decisions were no better than a coin toss: in 50% of cases, the smaller opportunity had a greater return. Shouldn't this consideration factor into your decision?
- Risk is also imprecisely measured. How does risk forecast error affect our sizing decisions?
- Most important of all, what is your objective?

Let us start with the last question. If your goal were to maximize expected returns *and* your expected returns forecasts were accurate, the investment decision would be straightforward: the portfolio would hold a single stock, the one with highest expected returns. Those who follow this rule need to read this book the most, but probably don't have enough money to buy it – poetic justice. A second decision criterion would be to maximize expected returns subject to a constraint on maximum tolerable risk, which in our analysis is described by portfolio volatility. While this seems an innocuous enough objective, it can result in very different rules. Some rules are right in theory and correct *ex ante*, but don't work as well *ex post*. I review the rules below, from simplest to most complex, and discuss their merit. In the following, we assume that the stocks are uncorrelated. This yields simple formulas, but also is the appropriate modeling framework when we think about idiosyncratic returns, since these are approximately uncorrelated.

We choose the sizing candidates based on three criteria. The first one is *simplicity*. The rules need only two inputs (at most): expected returns and volatilities, combined via simple ratios. The second one is *practical relevance*. The rules must be widely in use, if not in the fundamental investing community, in the quantitative one. Lastly, we require that the rules be *principled*.

The Proportional Rule. The simplest rule of all is the proportional rule. We build a portfolio of positions proportional to our buy-or-sell view. This rule ignores all but the essential information. The relative size of the conviction does not enter the sizing decision, neither does the volatility of the stock. An even simpler version of this rule, the "1/N" rule, simplifies the decision by sizing equally the longs and shorts. It has been analyzed in detail in [DeMiguel et al., 2009].

The Risk Parity (RP) Rule. If instead of equal sizing the position according to their gross market value, we size them so that their dollar idiosyncratic volatility is equal, then the GMV must be such that

$$(Gross\ Market\ Value)_i \times (\%\ idiosyncratic\ volatility)_i = (constant)$$

i.e., the GMV is proportional to the inverse of the stock's idiosyncratic volatility, and its side is determined by the long-short rule [Choueifaty and Coignard, 2008; Jurczenco, 2015].

The Mean-Variance (MV) Optimal Rule. Suppose that we want to have long or short theses for our stocks, and we want to construct a portfolio with the least idiosyncratic variance among those that meet a certain expected return. In this case, it can be shown that the single position is proportional to the inverse of the stock's idiosyncratic variance [Markowitz, 1959].

The Shrinked Mean-Variance (SMV) Optimal Rule. We also include a variant of the rule, in which we use minimum-variance allocation, but using modified idio variances. These variances are a weighted average of the stock's idio variance and the average stock idio variance in the sector at the time of the invested period. For example, a 25% shrinkage uses 75% of the stock's idio variance, and 25% of the industry's variance. The realized Sharpe Ratio is consistently higher for risk parity and for the proportional ratio than for the mean-variance. For more details on a justification for this approach, see Section 11.3.2 in the Appendix.

Procedure 6.2 Sizing alphas into positions.

For each stock in your universe with expected returns α, percentage idiosyncratic volatility σ, average sector volatility σ_{sector}, and shrinkage factor p between 0 and 1, use one of the following methods to set the target Net Market Value of the stock (NMV):

1. *Proportional: NMV* $= \kappa\alpha$
2. *Risk Parity: NMV* $= \kappa\alpha/\sigma$
3. *Mean Variance: NMV* $= \kappa\alpha/\sigma^2$
4. *Shrinked Mean Variance: NMV* $= \kappa\alpha/[p\sigma^2 + (1-p)\sigma^2_{\text{sector}}]$

Choose the constant κ so that the portfolio's GMV or the portfolio's volatility meets your predefined target.

6.4 ★Empirical Analysis of the Sizing Rules

Mean-Variance optimal portfolios have been a staple of financial theory since the mid-1960s, and it is tempting to adopt it uncritically. Markowitz himself set out to use the theory he helped develop and was actively involved in creating the Arbitrage Management Company in 1968. The naive application of the theory did not succeed, and the company was shut down after three years. It is part of financial lore that the mean-variance optimal portfolios resulted in highly unintuitive allocations, and that Markowitz himself eventually resorted to equal weighting. Many practitioners after Markowitz have witnessed firsthand somewhat unintuitive portfolios resulting from mean-variance portfolio construction, and the sometimes terrible performance that results from them. As early as 1971 [Frankfurter et al., 1971] and then again in 1980 [Jobson and Korkie, 1980] researchers observed that estimation error could wreak havoc on MVO portfolio construction. Perhaps it is easiest to think about this with the simplest case: you have an investment universe of 100 stocks with identical volatilities. To make things even simpler, the stocks have uncorrelated returns. You estimate the volatilities using daily returns over the past six months and size the positions using the MVO rule. You would

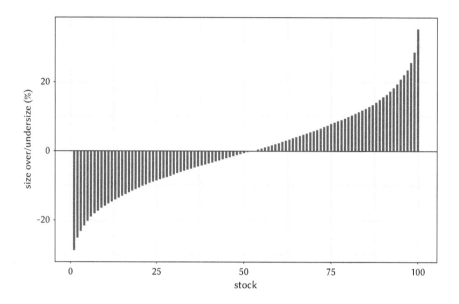

Figure 6.1   Position sizes in a simulated portfolio.

expect the positions to be equally sized, save for a small estimation error. Figure 6.1 shows the sizes of the stocks in the MVO, based on simulated data. The average oversizing or undersizing is about 9%. Eleven stocks have a mis-sizing in excess of 20%. The larger positions occur exactly where the error is bigger.

This is the best-case scenario: normal returns, independent, not changing over time. Reality is far messier: returns have heavier tails, experience regime changes, and have different volatilities. Under estimation for a low-volatility stock can result in a large position and a highly concentrated portfolio. Because of this, we should compare the performance of portfolios in more realistic scenarios. In order to evaluate performances in a realistic scenario, we perform a simple experiment. We use idiosyncratic returns for the period 1998–2019, and we restrict our focus to companies in the Russell 3000 with an average daily trading volume over the previous month of $2M or more. We split this twenty-two-year investment period into one-month investment horizons. At the beginning of every month, we generate alpha signals within each sector, with a positive cross-sectional correlation (5%) with the following one-month returns.

There are many ways to generate alpha signals, and we choose two:

1. Alpha signals drawn from a normal distribution. Empirically, PM-generated signals can be approximated with this distribution;
2. Simple buy/sell alpha signals with size equal to 1 or −1. These are at the other end of the spectrum, in the sense that there is no simpler way to describe a thesis. These signals ignore conviction.

We construct portfolios made of 50, 100 and 200 stocks using the four rules defined in Section 6.3, with unit Gross Market Value.[2] Then, we estimate the Sharpe Ratio of the three rules for each industry. We repeat the process over a large number of simulated alphas, and average the Sharpe Ratios. The results for gaussian signals are visualized in Figure 6.2, and for buy/sell signals are in Figure 6.3. The results are consistent across sectors and portfolio breadths. The simplest method – the proportional allocation rule – outperforms the others; in order: Mean Variance (Shrink 75%), Mean Variance (Shrink 50%), Risk Parity, Mean Variance (Shrink 25%), and Mean Variance.

Table 6.1 reports the relative improvement (averaged across sectors). The results are striking for two reasons. First, they show the impact that alpha sizing alone can have on the Sharpe Ratio. By choosing a method over a different one it is possible to gain or lose 10 to 30 points in relative risk-adjusted performance. Second, they call

Table 6.1 Sharpe Ratio for different rules based on *predicted* volatility, for portfolios of breadth of 100 stocks.

Method	Alpha		Loss	
	Gaussian	eq. w.	Gaussian	eq. w.
Proportional	1.61	1.29		
Mean Variance (shrink 75%)	1.55	1.23	−4%	−4%
Mean Variance (shrink 50%)	1.46	1.17	−9%	−9%
Risk Parity	1.46	1.16	−9%	−10%
Mean Variance (shrink 25%)	1.34	1.07	−16%	−17%
Mean Variance	1.07	0.83	−34%	−35%

---

[2] We also performed a test in which the portfolios had unit volatility and obtained similar results. We omit them for the sake of brevity.

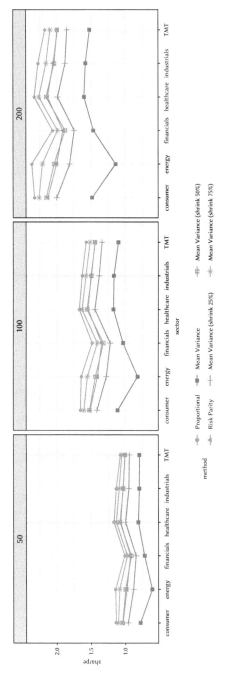

Figure 6.2 Realized Sharpe Ratios for sectors-based portfolio for portfolios of 50, 100 and 200 stocks, for the case of normally distributed signals.

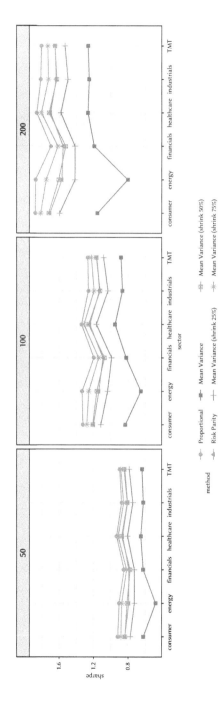

Figure 6.3 Realized Sharpe Ratios for sectors-based portfolio for portfolios of 50, 100 and 200 stocks, for case of buy/sell signals.

85

Table 6.2   Sharpe Ratio of different strategies using *realized* volatility, for portfolios of breadth of 100 stocks.

	Alpha		Loss	
Method	Gaussian	eq. w.	Gaussian	eq. w.
Proportional	1.61	1.29		
Mean Variance (shrink 75%)	1.45	1.16	−10%	−10%
Mean Variance (shrink 50%)	1.33	1.06	−18%	−18%
Risk Parity	1.30	1.04	−19%	−19%
Mean Variance (shrink 25%)	1.19	0.95	−26%	−27%
Mean Variance	0.86	0.68	−46%	−47%

into question the naive MV portfolio construction rule: the simple mean-variance rule performs considerably worse than the others: 34% and 35% for gaussian and buy/sell signals. Shrinked Mean-Variance with 75% of the weight assigned to the sector volatility performs quite close to the Proportional method. Why is this the case? One possibility is that estimation error of volatilities plays a role. To test if volatility estimation error is the issue, we do not use the predicted volatilities but instead the realized volatility during the investment month for which we created the portfolio. In other words, we have foresight of the coming-month volatilities, which we use in Procedure Box 6.2. The results are in Table 6.2, and do not change significantly when compared to those in Table 6.1. The real issue however lies with a different, subtle effect associated to any type of volatility scaling. To identify it, we cannot rely on historical data, but rather we generate a controlled experiment where the parameter under control is the *dispersion of stock volatilities in the investment universe.*

Here is an example. First, take a universe of one hundred stocks, all with volatilities equal to 25%. Then, consider another investment universe in which half the stocks have volatility of 40% and the other half have volatilities of 10%. We have forecasted expected returns for each of these stocks. Our forecast is noisy, so for each stock, the realized return is on average off by 5% compared to the forecast. In the case of the first investment universe, mistakes carry the same costs across all stocks, because they have all the same volatilities, and therefore their sizes are determined by their expected returns only. In the case of the second investment universe, however, costs are borne asymmetrically. Low-volatility stocks are sized higher than high-vol ones; in fact, much higher in the case of Mean-Variance scaling. If we make a mistake of 5% in the expected return forecast on a low-volatility stock, we pay a much higher cost than if we make the same mistake on the high-volatility one. The average NMV misallocation due to forecast error on the first universe, using the Mean-Variance Rule, is $0.05/0.25^2 = 0.8$. The average NMV misallocation in the second universe is $(1/2) \times 0.05/0.10^2 + (1/2) * 0.05/0.40^2 = 2.65$, a 332% increase!

In summary, it is not the volatility estimation error that matters, but rather the estimation error of the expected returns, combined with the fact there is variation in volatilities across the stock universe. To underscore this fact, in Table 6.3 I show the results of a more realistic simulation, in which the stock volatilities average 34% and have increasing dispersion. I run 4000 simulations of returns for one hundred stocks over a period of 3 years. Stocks have average volatility of 30%, but we allow for volatilities to vary across stocks; e.g., in one simulation, some stocks have a volatility of 28% and some have a volatility of 40%. The standard deviation of volatilities across stocks is displayed in the first column of the table and characterizes the heterogeneity of the population of securities. Variances are estimated over a period of 63 trading days. The portfolios are unit-variance, and their realized Sharpe Ratios is displayed in columns 2–5. In addition to the mean-variance allocation, I am adding yet another rule: the "exact mean-variance allocation". This is the allocation when the stock volatility is known exactly, without any estimation error. The difference in Sharpe Ratio between MV and MV_{exact} is only due to this additional knowledge, and it is minimal. The results confirm the intuition from our toy model of stock volatilities. When volatilities

Table 6.3 Results of simulated strategies using different sizing methods.

std.dev. of stock	Proportional	Risk Parity	MV	MV_{exact}
0.0	3.5	3.5	3.5	3.5
7.8	3.5	3.4	3.0	3.1
18.0	3.4	3.0	2.1	2.1
33.8	3.3	2.5	1.1	1.2

across stocks are identical, the Sharpe Ratio is identical across methods. As dispersion increases, the Proportional rule pulls away, the Risk Parity one degrades less, and the Mean-Variance – with or without foresight – underperforms. This long section boils down to a simple recommendation, highlighted in Insight 6.2:

Insight 6.2 Sizing heuristic.

Using target positions that are proportional to the forecasted expected returns of a stock beats other common methods.

6.5 From Ideas to Positions

I have omitted an important step in the process of translating fundamental ideas into positions. Say that you have estimated the expected returns for a small portfolio shown in Table 6.4 and want to convert it into a portfolio. The NMVs are just the expected returns times 15.8, so that the GMV of the portfolio matches a target level of $315M. The problem with this simple scaling is that the portfolio will have factor risk, possibly quite a lot of it. For example, say that this portfolio has a market beta of $15M, and a momentum exposure of $25M. We would like to have a simple way to modify our investment ideas as little as possible, while attaining zero factor risk. I should emphasize that this is a good first take to turn your "raw" ideas into factor-neutral ideas. It is the first word, but not necessarily the last one. One consideration to keep in mind is that transaction costs can affect sizing. Another consideration is that perhaps being rigidly factor-neutral is a bit too demanding. If you consider this procedure as a "rule of thumb" to compute factor-neutral sizings, you will find this very useful. In addition, it is a simple procedure, which you can implement in Excel.

The problem we are solving is, in words, the following:

Find modified positions that minimize distance from your original convictions such that the positions have zero factor exposures and GMV equal to your target GMV.

A variant of this problem requires that, instead of meeting a certain GMV requirement, we meet a certain expected volatility

Table 6.4 Expected returns and NMV.

Stock	Expected Return (%)	NMV
ADBE	7.8	123.3
MSFT	−0.8	−13.2
CSCO	2.4	38.2
IBM	−5.3	−83.5
NVDA	0.3	5.0
INTC	−3.3	−51.9

requirement. The solution to these two problems is in the Appendix, Section 11.4. You do not need to know the details: the procedure is detailed in Procedure Box 6.3.

Procedure 6.3 Sizing alphas into positions, with zero factor risk.

You are given a factor loadings matrix **B** with a number of rows equal to the number of stocks in the estimation universe (e.g., 2000 for the US), and a number of columns equal to the number of factors. The expected returns are collected in a vector α. You have a known target GMV for your portfolio.

1. Regress the column α against the columns of **B**. In formulas: $\alpha = \mathbf{B}\mathbf{x} + \epsilon$. The vector ϵ is the vector of residuals of the linear regression.
2. Standardize the vector ϵ: $a_i = \epsilon_i / \sum_i |\epsilon_i|$. Here the index i denotes the i-th stock in your portfolio.
3. Set the NMV of stock i to $NMV_i = a_i \times GMV$.

6.6   Time-Series Risk-Based Portfolio Targeting

Decisions about sizing are decisions about volatility. When you size a portfolio on a given day, you size the volatility of each individual position. Volatility allocation decisions don't occur only at a point in time; they also occur over time. You make decisions about the overall portfolio size day by day. Your portfolio's GMV varies slightly daily as a result of tactical trading: opening a position; adjusting a conviction level; or closing a trade that has reached its end of life. However, in the absence of exceptional events, it stays range-bound. These exceptional events include additional capital allocation to a fund or to a portfolio, and also the occurrence of losses large enough to justify a large defensive reduction.[3] Aside from these rare events, what should we target? Gross Market Value is one option, but not the only one. An alternative would be to target the volatility of the portfolio. GMV and volatility targeting are by far the two most common options adopted by practitioners and the latter has recently attracted the attention of academics as well [Moreira and Muir, 2017, 2019; Harvey et al., 2018]. Compared to GMV targeting, volatility targeting has one obvious benefit, and a potential non-obvious one. The obvious benefit is that portfolio volatility is a better measure of risk than GMV. Say that you want to compare the risk of your portfolio over time, and your GMV is constant at $1B in the first half of 2020. Was the risk of the portfolio the same in January as it was in March? Obviously not! The volatility of the same portfolio, seen through the lens of its predicted volatility, would have shown a much increased risk in March, and this information would have been both somewhat correct and useful to the manager. Yet, a portfolio manager is not compensated for volatility management. Should you care about it if it reduced your profitability? This is where the second benefit may come in. The hypothesis we want to test is that volatility targeting may increase the Sharpe Ratio and/or the return on GMV of the strategy. The mechanism by which this may happen is simple. Volatility is persistent over time. A week of high volatility is likely to be followed by a day of high volatility, the same for a volatile month. This means that volatility is predictable to some extent. PnL, however, does not appear to be predictable for fundamental strategies. High PnL today does not portend high PnL tomorrow. If that is the case, then if we reduce the volatility back to its target level when it spikes, it should allow you to navigate the risk of the portfolio in the near future, without affecting its profitability much. Many things could disprove this story, however. First, by reducing volatility and GMV, we may affect the magnitude

---

[3] I devote Chapter 9 to this subject.

of PnL; second, large volatility spikes are associated to PnL losses. What if PnL is reverting? Then, the chain of events would be

$$(volatility\ increase) \to (PnL\ loss) \to (volatility\ reduction)$$
$$\to (smaller\ PnL\ gain\ due\ to\ derisking)$$

We need at least some empirical confirmation that the volatility targeting story holds. To this effect, we focus on the idiosyncratic volatility of the portfolio, in the spirit of the separation of concerns we discussed at the beginning of the chapter. We test both GMV and volatility targeting under many designs:

1. Using normal signals and buy/sell signals;
2. With signals one month ahead and three months ahead. The goal of longer-term signals is to allow for PnL reversion in the aftermath of a volatility spike;
3. On portfolios of different breadth: 50, 100, and 200 stocks;
4. For each sector.

For each combination signal type/signal horizon/breadth/sector, we run 50 simulations for the period 1998–2019 on US stocks; in the simulations, GMV and volatilities are targeted on a daily basis. An objection to such a daily procedure is that it could be too time-consuming and expensive. It is, however, a good approximation; monthly targeting, for example, yielded similar results (I am omitting these simulations for the sake of brevity).

The results for normal signals are shown in Figure 6.4, and for buy/sell signals in Figure 6.5. Each plot in the grid shows the Sharpe Ratio (y axis) for each sector (x axis), for GMV and volatility targeting. The grid controls for the breadth of the portfolio (columns) and fore-casting horizon of the alphas (rows). The results are very consistent: for every signal type, horizon, sector, and portfolio breadth, volatility targeting generates higher risk-adjusted returns. There is variation across sectors, though, and this variation matters to PMs, who are usually covering individual sectors. Tables 6.5 and 6.6 show the Sharpe Ratios of GMV and volatility targeting strategies, for both monthly and quarterly forecasting horizons. The improvement is higher for TMT and financials. We can confirm the benefits of time-series volatility targeting, and we summarize in Procedure Box 6.3.

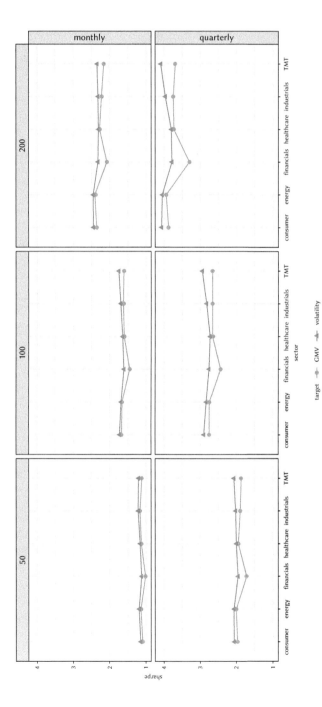

Figure 6.4 Realized Sharpe for the case of normally distributed signals.

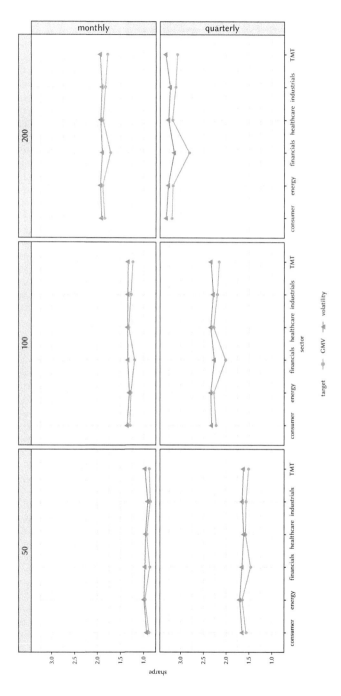

Figure 6.5 Realized Sharpe for the case of buy/sell signals.

Table 6.5 Sharpe Ratio of unit-GMV and unit-dollar volatility scaling, with one-month-ahead forecasts and gaussian and buy-sell signal.

Sector	Buy/Sell			Gaussian		
	GMV	vol	vol % gain	GMV	vol	% vol gain
consumer	1.29	1.34	3.9	1.61	1.67	3.9
energy	1.35	1.38	2.4	1.63	1.68	2.8
financials	1.14	1.27	11.5	1.47	1.62	10.6
healthcare	1.32	1.36	2.7	1.60	1.64	2.2
industrials	1.26	1.32	4.3	1.60	1.68	5.3
TMT	1.17	1.30	10.3	1.51	1.62	6.9

Table 6.6 Sharpe Ratio of unit-GMV and unit-dollar volatility scaling, with one-quarter-ahead forecasts and gaussian and buy-sell signal.

Sector	Buy/Sell			Gaussian		
	GMV	vol	vol % gain	GMV	vol	% vol gain
consumer	0.71	0.7	4.2	0.93	0.97	4.7
energy	0.74	0.77	4.7	0.98	1.01	3.3
financials	0.69	0.77	11.2	0.85	0.95	12.0
healthcare	0.73	0.75	3.1	0.92	0.97	5.2
industrials	0.75	0.78	4.1	0.91	0.98	7.5
TMT	0.78	0.81	4.0	0.88	0.96	8.1

Insight 6.3 Benefits of Volatility Targeting.

Targeting Volatility has two benefits:

1. It controls for risk and maximum losses better than GMV targeting;
2. It results in higher risk-adjusted performance.

Volatility is persistent and partially predictable, while PnL has no strong relationship to volatility. *Not* targeting volatility doesn't take advantage of the fact that we can predict that future volatility will be high if current volatility is high.

6.7   ★Frequently Asked Questions About Performance

Q: *How do I convert the Sharpe Ratio computed on daily returns to an Annualized Sharpe?*

A: From the earlier question: the annualized volatility of a strategy is equal to

$$\sqrt{252} \times (daily\ volatility)$$

The annualized return of a strategy is $252 \times (daily\ return)$. Putting the two together:

$$
\begin{aligned}
Sharpe_{annualized} &= \frac{(annualized\ return)}{(annualized\ volatility)} \\[2mm]
&= \frac{252 \times (daily\ return)}{\sqrt{252} \times (annualized\ volatility)} \\[2mm]
&= \sqrt{252}\,\frac{(daily\ return)}{(daily\ volatility)} \\[2mm]
&= \sqrt{252} \times Sharpe_{daily}
\end{aligned}
$$

A similar calculation holds for conversion from weekly to annual:

$$Sharpe_{annualized} = \sqrt{52} \times Sharpe_{weekly}$$

Q: *How Reliable is the estimate of my Sharpe Ratio? Shouldn't you provide a confidence band?*

A: Yes, the estimate of Sharpe Ratio is imprecise, and it is possible to estimate confidence intervals. The interval depends on the assumptions you make about returns; a convenient reference is [Lo, 2002]. A simple formula for the approximate 95% confidence interval on the annualized Sharpe Ratio is the following:

$(Sharpe\ Ratio) = (Sharpe\ Ratio\ Estimate)$

$$\pm\, 1.96 \sqrt{\frac{1 + (1/2)(Sharpe\ Ratio\ Estimate)^2}{(number\ of\ observations)}}$$

The term $\sqrt{1 + (1/2)(SR\ Estimate)^2/(\#\ of\ obs.)}$ is the *Standard Error of the Sharpe Ratio*. Let's make a concrete example.

Suppose you have a three-year history of daily returns (756 trading days). The daily Sharpe Ratio is 0.1; see above for the relationship between daily and annualized Sharpe Ratios. The Standard Error is $\sqrt{(1 + 0.1^2/2)/756} = 0.036$. If we annualized the Sharpe Ratio and the Standard Error, we obtain a Sharpe Ratio of 1.6 and an s.e. of 0.6. The 95% confidence interval is $(1.6 - 1.2, 1.6 + 1.2) = (0.4, 2.8)$.

6.8   Takeaway Messages

1. Separate in your mind factor and idiosyncratic returns; specifically, think about the role of market and industry returns on the stocks you cover. When estimating target returns, think about *idiosyncratic returns*.
2. For each stock in your universe, develop a view on its *expected idiosyncratic* return $\bar{r}$ at a certain investment horizon T (e.g., 10% at 2 months);
3. Convert all the expected returns to the same investment horizon by dividing the return by the horizon: $\alpha = \bar{r}/T$.
4. Convert expected returns into factor-neutral expected returns:
   a. Regress the column α against the columns of the loadings matrix $\mathbf{B}$. In formulas: $\alpha = \mathbf{B}x + \epsilon$. The vector ϵ is the vector of residuals of the linear regression.
   b. Standardize the vector ϵ: $a_i = \epsilon_i/\sum_i |\epsilon_i|$. Here the index i denotes the i-th stock in your portfolio.

   This step ensures that the impact of factor bets on portfolio returns is eliminated.
5. Convert orthogonal alphas into single-position NMVs, by choosing one of two rules:
   a. *Proportional rule:* set the NMV of stock i to $NMV_i = a_i \times$ (*target GMV*).

b. *Shrinked Mean Variance:* set the NMV of stock i to $NMV_i = \kappa a_i / [p\sigma_i^2 + (1-p)\sigma_{\text{sector}}^2]$ with κ such that the total GMV meets the target requirement.

In practice, the simplest rule (proportional) may be preferable, especially in sector-focused portfolios.

6. Over time, scale the GMV of the portfolio so that the predicted dollar idiosyncratic volatility of the portfolio matches a given target. Volatility targeting improves risk-adjusted performance.

Chapter 7

Manage Factor Risk

- *What will you learn here:* Three things. First, how to easily adjust portfolio positions in order to reduce factor risk. Second, how to think about risk parameters and risk limits. Lastly, how to plan for systematic portfolio construction in order to achieve greater execution efficiency and investment productivity.
- *Why do you need it:* Because, in the majority of cases, portfolio management is an interactive process. You will act on your portfolio when risk is unacceptably high, and to do it, you will need to know what "unacceptably high" risk is, and how to bring it to an acceptable level. You *will* need some systematic portfolio construction when your strategy becomes sufficiently big and complex.
- *When will you need this:* You will use tactical portfolio management daily; you will perform portfolio optimization

occasionally (say, once a month or less). You will set risk limits rarely (less often than once a year), but will need to understand and embrace them once and for all – an important step. Maybe you will never need systematic portfolio construction tools. But when the time comes, they will be *the only* thing you need, until they are in place.

7.1   Tactical Factor Risk Management

If you are a fundamental investor, factor returns are the cross-currents that can wreak your portfolio. A recurrent theme in this book is that, as soon as your portfolio is sufficiently broad (say, more than 50 stocks), you should not have large factor exposures or carry large factor risks. There are several reasons for this. First, you don't have any edge in investing in factors. Factor investing is a well-developed domain, with specialized players, and even for them, attaining good performance is very challenging. Secondly, factor models enable you to put in practice an important design principle used by engineers: *separation of concerns*. Performance can be decomposed into systematic and idiosyncratic components. Most importantly, these components are investable. To a large degree, you can invest in one or the other and if you invest in a mix of both, you can separate your portfolio into a systematic and idiosyncratic one. Focusing on one – the idiosyncratic part – allows you to achieve greater clarity about your investing decision, better diagnosis and adaptation when things don't go as expected, which is most of the time. Lastly: your investors are not paying you to replicate the market, ride momentum, or short already shorted stocks. You may have to do sometimes all of the above, but not all the time. Your fiduciary duty toward investors requires that you focus on performance that is independent of factors.

   We don't live a factor-free world. The first step is to be able to see the factors. We do this by decomposing the volatility of our portfolios. Factor PnL is the sum of all the individual factor PnLs; each factor PnL is the product of factor exposure and factor return; and each factor exposure is the sumproduct of loadings and position NMVs. In formulas:

$$\text{PnL} = \text{idio PnL}+ \qquad\qquad\qquad\qquad (7.1)$$

factor PnL

$\downarrow$ $\searrow$

factor PnL_1 $+\text{factor PnL}_2 + ...$

$\downarrow$

$\$\text{exposure}_1 \times \text{factor return}_1$ $+\text{factor PnL}_2 + ...$

$\downarrow$ $\searrow$

$(\beta_{11} \times \text{NMV}_1 + ...) \times \text{factor return}_1$ $+\text{factor PnL}_2 + ...$

The factor dollar exposures drive the systematic performance of your portfolio. Not surprisingly, they also drive its systematic risk. This is expedient, because the set of the dollar exposures of your portfolio is usually small compared to the size of a portfolio. If you are a sector specialist, then you will have exposure only to some style factors and a handful of industries in your sector: 10–15 factors, compared to 80–150 for the portfolio positions themselves. If you are a generalist, or manage a business, then the exposures will be in styles, industries, maybe a few countries. These may be as many as 100 exposures, but the portfolio may contain 1000 positions or more. What is more important is that not all exposures are created equal. Some matter much more than others both for risk and return. In practice, you will follow closely no more than 10 factors. In order to determine which ones, and to quantify their relative impact, we use an analytical tool called portfolio risk decomposition.

In Table 7.1 I show an example for a technology-focused portfolio. Below is the interpretation of each column:

- *%Var*. This is the percentage of total variance for every group, subgroup, and individual factor. Why variance and not volatility? The reason is that the variance of the sum of two *independent* returns is equal to the sum of variance of independent returns, as you may recall from Chapter 1. When partitioning risk, variance "adds up" and is therefore a more useful metric. The main groups are idio and total, and sum up to 100%. The subgroups are style and industry,

Table 7.1 An example of risk decomposition for a technology sector portfolio.

	%Var	$Exp	$Vol	MCFR
TOTAL	100		14.1	
IDIO	85		13.0	
FACTOR	15		5.5	
STYLE	7.6		3.8	
Country	0	1	0.0	−0.37
12 Mo Momentum	5.05	−320	3.11	−5.76
Market Sensitivity	0.75	−124	1.24	−2.20
Volatility	0.16	−56	0.57	−1.03
Earnings Yield	0.13	−40	0.40	−1.21
Value	0.06	25	0.25	0.86
Growth	0.12	52	0.52	0.84
Profitability	0.23	63	0.63	1.32
Short Interest	0.30	81	0.81	1.34
HF Ownership	0.50	85	0.86	2.14
INDUSTRY	7.4		392	
Software	0.88	131	1.31	2.46
Comm. Equip.	1.32	154	1.54	3.12
Electronic HW	5.38	329	3.25	5.96
Semi HW	0.12	−33	3.36	−1.34

their percentage of total variance sum up to 15%. The individual factors also sum up to 15%, and they describe the percentage of total risk that can be attributed to each of them. However, you may notice that the style factors sum to 7.3%, which is slightly different than the 7.6% of style risk. The reason is that style and industry factors are slightly positively correlated. Industry and Style are no longer independent; their joint variance does not add up. One way to take this into account is to split the increase in variance and split it equally in the attribution between the two groups.[1]

How to use this information: this columns helps you focus your information on what matters, from an aggregated level to a very disaggregated one. How "pure" is my portfolio? The percentage of

---

[1] One minor technical note: the "%Var" decomposition varies slightly among vendors. Some include the correlation contributions, some don't. The results are not very sensitive to this choice.

idio variance will help you answer this question.[2] The next question is: Where is factor risk coming from? In this case, it's in equal parts style and industry. Say that you have put on conscious industry bets and are comfortable with the risk. Now you focus on style risk. What is its main driver? The answer is easy: 12-Month Momentum is the main contributor. Now you know what to look for.

- *$Exposure and $Vol.* This is the dollar exposure (in $M) for all factors, and the volatility, expressed in annualized dollars.[3]

  How to use this information: the risk of each factor is proportional to its dollar exposure, via the relationship (factor risk) = (factor exposure) × (factor vol); you can easily estimate the reduction in factor vol resulting from cutting exposure. If 12-Month Momentum has a $Vol of $3.11M at current exposure level, cutting it by 50% will bring it to $1.55M. A second use of exposures is for scenario analysis.

- *MCFR.* This is the *Marginal Contribution to Factor Risk.* Consider 12-Month Momentum. We want to reduce its exposure by $10M. The current factor risk is $5.5M. By how much will factor risk be reduced? The answer is 5.76 × 10 = $57.6K (notice that the reduction is in thousands of dollars). In other words, 5.76 is the reduction (in thousands of dollars) in factor risk resulting from the reduction in 12-Month Momentum exposure of $1M.

  How to use this information: while the %Var and $Vol give us measures of average factor contribution of each factor to total factor risk, the MCFR tells us what to do to reduce it. This is especially true when we are concerned about specific factors, or groups of factors. *If* we have large risk in value and growth, *and* we fear a change in sentiment or in macroeconomic fundamentals, e.g., a steepening of the yield curve, *then* we need to know the impact of our corrective actions. That is the role of the MCFR.

We are not yet done in our quest to tame factor risk. We don't trade factor exposures[4]; we trade stocks. We need a second stock screener.

---

[2] For the more fundamental question, "How high should my % idio variance be?", see the end of the chapter.

[3] To convert to a monthly, weekly or daily volatility, divide by $\sqrt{12} \simeq 3.5$ and $\sqrt{52} \simeq$ 7.2 or $\sqrt{252} \simeq 16$, respectively (see Section 4.2).

[4] Or better, we don't trade them *yet.* We will see in a later section how hedging achieves exactly this.

Table 7.2 Per-stock Net Market Value (in $M), Marginal Contribution to Factor Risk, 12-Month Momentum loading, and recommended action.

Stock	NMV	MCFR	12-Mo Mo	Action
ADBE	123.3	−0.4	−0.32	BUY
MSFT	−13.2	0.3	1	SELL SHORT
CSCO	38.2	0.5	.5	REDUCE
IBM	−83.5	1.4	0.25	SELL SHORT
NVDA	5.0	−0.12	1.2	DO NOT TRADE
INTC	−51.9	−2.3	−0.52	COVER
...	...	...	...	...

Say that we focus on 12-Month Momentum as a secondary criterion for action. We may want to focus on this factor for two reasons:

1. The absolute size of its dollar exposure exceeds our predefined guideline for this factor. More on single-factor limits is in Section 7.2.4;
2. The contribution to factor risk of 12-Month Momentum is very high, relative to that of other factors. Table 7.1 shows that this is the case in our example: 12-Month Momentum contributes 5.05% to total variance.

Table 7.2 contains the relevant information.[5] The table further expands the risk decomposition at the stock level. Every stock has a marginal impact on the portfolio's factor risk. We have now the essential tools to structure a portfolio, summarized in Procedure Box 7.1.

Procedure 7.1 Tactical portfolio construction.

1. Start with a set of fundamental theses (Section 6.2).
2. Convert these theses into a dollar position using Procedure 6.2.

(continued)

---

[5] As noted before, this information may be presented in a different format in your analytical tool of choice.

(*Continued*)

3. Perform a risk decomposition.
4. If the percentage of idio variance is low, identify the group of factors responsible for it. For guidance regarding acceptable levels of factor risk, see Section 7.2.1.
5. Identify the largest factor or factors responsible for the low percentage; and include factors that have exposures exceeding the single-factor exposures, as discussed in Section 7.2.4.
6. Finally, identify the trades by asset that both reduce overall factor risk and the specific factor exposure. Choose trades compatibly with your fundamental convictions, and with your goals to reduce or increase the Gross Market Value of the portfolio.
7. Change the positions in a direction that is (a) compatible with your convictions; (b) reducing factor risk to an acceptable level; (c) reducing exposures to individual factors that you are currently targeting.

7.1.1   Optimize If You Must

Portfolios get out of shape occasionally. Here are a few examples of how this could happen:

- There is a large, unmistakable factor: "rotation". This happens when certain factors exhibit large drawdowns or run-ups. As a result, the volatilities of the factors are updated to account for the large spikes. Because the factor volatility changes, factor risk changes. Moreover, for certain factors like momentum and short interest, the loadings can change abruptly as well: A 12-month loser stock has a fast recovery; a heavily shorted stock is "squeezed" (the short holders are forced to cover to avoid incurring excessive losses). Some of the most prominent events occurred on August 8–11, 2007, August–December 2008, February 22–March 4, 2016, October 8–December 1, 2018, and, of course, February 22–March 19, 2020. The combination of changes in factor risk and exposures can force a PM to take decisive action on the portfolio.

- There are periods in which the alpha identified by PMs is strong and persistent. This is good news! However, this also implies that certain factors will blow out of proportion. Long- and medium-term momentum exposures will grow because the book is long winners and short losers; beta and volatility factor exposures are likely to grow as well. These exposures portend danger. Momentum especially can experience a crash in the event of a market rebound. The most prominent such episode is the first half of 2009 (and, for some PMs, the last quarter of 2008): books were profitable in this period, but risk management was particularly demanding.

- On a slightly less epic scale, earnings season can be hard to manage as well. The strongest convictions precede earnings. Although they are idiosyncratic in nature, they can be caught in the cross-winds of large and unexpected factor returns. It can happen that unintentionally the portfolio may take on way too much factor risk.

- Lastly, you will on occasion pay attention to *custom factors*. These are the subject of Section 8.4. From a qualitative standpoint, these will show up in your process as loadings, i.e., stock characteristics, that incorporate nonstandard information. A popular example is given by ESG (Environment, Governance and Sustainability) scores.

The goal of tactical portfolio optimization is to bring a portfolio back to acceptable risk levels, when doing so by trading a few stocks directionally is not sufficient. If finding an acceptable trade becomes too time-consuming, chances are that the proposed trade itself may be far from optimal. The optimization formulation must extend the simple trade-heuristics of the previous section without becoming unwieldy. We need to introduce custom factor loadings, which are qualitatively like risk model factor loadings. As part of the optimization problem, we want to be able to impose bounds on the final portfolio exposures to both risk model and custom factors. In addition to these constraints, there are two constraints that are necessary to obtain a meaningful solution. The first one is a constraint on the maximum tolerable factor risk. The second one is a constraint on the minimum "size" of the portfolio. Without this constraint, the optimizer would choose to reduce dollar factor exposures and factor risk by simply "shrinking" the portfolio – an undesirable outcome. "Size" constraints, however, are not straightforward. It seems natural to want a portfolio with a *minimum* total risk. It turns out that finding an "optimal" portfolio with this requirement is as computationally intensive as it gets.[6] Therefore, we cannot use this constraint. An alternative is to have a constraint on the minimum Gross Market Value of the portfolio. This is a problem that can be solved and that has an obvious relationship to the size of the portfolio. We have left for last the objective function. As a standard problem formulation, the most natural choice is to *minimize the expected transaction cost*. Summing up, the problem can be qualitatively formulated as follows:

min (*transaction cost*)

s.t. (*final exposures are bounded*)

(*final custom exposures are bounded below and/or above*)

(*factor risk is bounded below and/or above*)

(*GMV is bounded below*)

I describe the quantitative formulation in Section 11.7 of the Appendix. The output of the optimization should include at least these data:

- Trade vector, with cost per trade.
- Total t-cost.
- Distance from starting portfolio (see below for definition).
- Initial and final portfolio total, idio, and factor volatility.
- Initial and final %idiovar.
- Initial and final GMV.

This is of course not the only optimization formulation. At the very least, I believe it would be useful to consider alternatives to the transaction cost minimization. These are especially useful when the transaction costs are low. The single most insightful change to the optimization is to replace the objective function of the optimization with a "distance" from the starting portfolio, defined as the sum of the squared NMVs of the individual trades. Alternatively, the distance can be defined as the "idiosyncratic tracking error", defined as the idiosyncratic variance of the trade vector.

---

[6] In technical terms, a quadratic program with a single "greater than" constraint on risk is NP-hard; see [Pardalos and Vavasis, 1991].

7.2   Strategic Factor Risk Management

Tactical management is of little use without policies for long-term risk. These policies should set limits to risk in a principled, yet intuitive way. The next sections tell you all you wanted to know about risk limits:[7]

- What should my maximum factor risk be?
- I would like to keep some market exposure, but how much is too much? What would be different if I worked in a multi-manager platform?
- How should I reason about single-stock holdings?
- Should there be single-factor exposures? And how big?

7.2.1   Setting an Upper Limit on Factor Risk

The analysis so far is about principles, tools and processes. However, we have not discussed parameters and guidelines. Among them, perhaps the most important decision regards the amount of factor risk to hold in the portfolio. We could express this decision by requiring that factor return volatility be no more than a maximum percentage of the volatility of the portfolio. However, usually the guideline is expressed by practitioners in a different way. Factor returns and idiosyncratic returns are uncorrelated; as we saw in the previous chapter, the variance of their sum (i.e., the variance of the portfolio's returns) is equal to the sum of the individual variances (variances of independent returns "add up"; volatilities don't). So, we say that factor *variance* should not be more than a certain percentage of the portfolio variance. For example, say that the annual volatility of your portfolio is $10M and the limit as percentage of total variance is 20%. Then the maximum factor return variance is $0.2 * (\$10M)^2 = \$20M^2$ (yes, squared million $). The maximum factor volatility is $4.5M (or, $\sqrt{(20)}$).

What should be the right percentage? There are no right answers, only trade-offs; let us make them explicit. The intuition is that, if you allow too much factor variance in your portfolio, your risk-adjusted performance will degrade, because you have no control over a fraction of your PnL. And a lower risk-adjusted performance means, among other things, a lower leverage ratio (I will go over this in detail in

---

[7] But were afraid to ask.

a later question). Beyond the intuition, we should try to understand the relationship between idio variance percentage and risk-adjusted performance. We introduce a few definitions:

- The *% idio variance* (which we also denote *p*) is the ratio between a portfolio's idio variance and total variance:

$$\% \; idiovar = \frac{idio \; var}{total \; var}$$

- The *Information Ratio* (IR) is the ratio between a portfolio's expected idiosyncratic PnL and its idio volatility.

We *assume* that a fundamental portfolio manager has no skill in factors. This is not true a priori; but empirically, most PMs have no skill in style factors whatsoever, and a few have very moderate skills in having exposures to industries or sectors. So we'll go with this and say that the expected total PnL of a portfolio is just equal to its idio PnL. In reality, the volatility of a portfolio is higher than its idio volatility alone. Given these assumptions, the relationship between IR, SR and *p* is

$$\frac{Information \; Ratio - Sharpe \; Ratio}{Information \; Ratio} = 1 - \sqrt{\% \; idiovar}$$

So the Sharpe Ratio degrades when there is factor risk. By how much? Table 7.3 and Figure 7.1 provide some numerical examples. The rule of thumb is that *for every 5 points reduction in idio variance, you experience a relative reduction in performance of about 2.5 points.* That is for the same volatility budget, you will experience a PnL 2.5% lower, on average. Another way to see this: a lower *p* means that you can have lower leverage, since your SR is reduced.

   Given all of this, what is not to like about a 100% idio variance? At least three things.

- First, keeping a book at 100% idio is costly. It has a *cognitive cost* to size the positions so that all sources of systematic risk are neutralized. And it has a *financial cost* in that it requires more trading, and therefore higher trading costs. For a large portfolio, these costs can exceed 5% of the total PnL. We ignored them in our analysis.

Table 7.3 Risk-adjusted losses for keeping a percentage of idio variance below 100% of total variance.

Idiovar (%)	IR degradation (%)
95	2.5
90	5.1
85	7.8
80	10.6
75	13.4

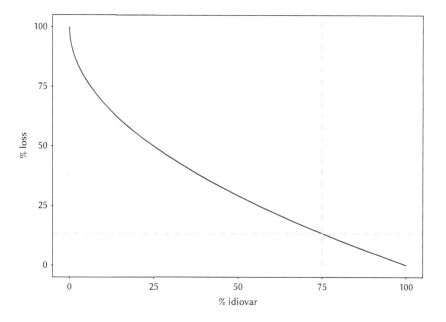

Figure 7.1 Relationship between percentage idio var and risk-adjusted performance degradation.

- Secondly, keeping a book at 100% may interfere with sizing decisions. If the PM believes she has significant sizing skills, and she finds that adjusting the portfolio affects the pristine sizes to a large extent, then she will give away idiosyncratic PnL. Otherwise stated: we assumed that idio PnL did not depend on factor PnL, but in reality it does, somewhat.

- Lastly: by keeping the book at 100%, we may be precisely wrong, rather than approximately right. We assumed that we have a risk model telling us the "true" factor risk of the portfolio. Real-world models are far, *far* from the truth. Even state-of-the-art models can predict widely different percentage idio variances for a portfolio, typically 5–10 points, and they all claim to be right! And they all claim to be 5% better than the previous generation. We may be managing to noise *just a bit*.

Insight 7.1 Minimum percent idio variance.

There are diminishing returns to having higher idio variance. Beyond 75%, the benefits of higher idio variance percentage may be offset by higher costs.

Given all these considerations, what is the right p? If you are really targeting idio returns, and have access to a good risk model, it's hard to argue against a p lower than 75%, especially if the factor risk is originated by well-known, uncontroversial factors, like market, long-term momentum, volatility factor, and (at least) sector factors. Provided that you have little or no exposure to these vanilla factors and are above 75%, ask yourself these questions:

- Do you *need* to leverage your strategy very high? The higher the leverage, the lower the tolerance for factor risk.
- Do you have narrow portfolios (few stocks)? Narrow portfolios are harder to manage to a high p.
- Do you have widely different levels of conviction in your positions and/or sizing skill? The stronger your belief in your sizing, the fewer the degrees of freedom in managing to a high p.
- Do you have access to tools like optimizers and quantitative experts to help with portfolio construction? If so, your cognitive costs are reduced and you can afford a higher p.
- Do you trade in illiquid stocks? If so, the cost of managing to the book to a high p could be prohibitive, and the risk model itself may be less accurate.

- Do you always make money, irrespective of portfolio construction? If so, you don't really need to care about p. But I want to be your best friend forever.

7.2.2 Setting a Limit on Market Exposure

If you are running a portfolio with few stocks and/or have mediocre Sharpe, you should have some exposure to the market. If you have a broad portfolio (over a thousand stocks) and a Sharpe of 1.5 or more, then you are better off running market-neutral. There are two competing considerations at play:

1. Portfolio managers express their fundamental views, and it is only natural that they are occasionally slightly long or short the market. This exposure is just a consequence of their fundamental views, and forcing them to be market-neutral would distort their sizes and/or take too much effort;
2. The market has positive Sharpe, and we should be exposed to it. If we want to be cynical, we are being paid a healthy slope for returns that an investor could buy elsewhere for just a few bps.

The first one is easier to dispel. For starters, it is very easy to stay market neutral. Even if you have some illiquid stocks, it is trivial when you have more than 20 stocks in your portfolio. Oftentimes, the exposure comes from a lack of conviction in the shorts. Sometimes you, the PM, come from a long-only shop. Whichever the reason, if you believe in betting on relative value, and cover enough stocks, managing market-neutral is consistent with this idea and is easy. If you happen to have some temporary market exposure, that can be hedged inexpensively.

The second one is trickier. The approach I recommend is to characterize the "best" proportion of market exposure. If you receive a volatility budget, then your goal is to maximize the risk-adjusted performance, because this allows you to achieve the highest possible PnL. When you are allowed to have market exposure, you are allowed to invest in two assets. The first one is your portfolio in market-neutral form, which has Sharpe Ratio Sharpe_{port}; the other is the market, with Sharpe Ratio Sharpe_m. The two have nearly uncorrelated returns.

The optimal ratio can be expressed in various forms:[8]

- The optimal percentage variance allocated to the market is

$$\frac{market\ variance}{total\ variance} = \frac{1}{1 + \left(\frac{(Sharpe\ Ratio)_{port}}{(Sharpe\ Ratio)_m}\right)^2}$$

The higher your Sharpe, the lower the exposure to the market. Example: if your portfolio has Sharpe 1.5 and you assume that the market has Sharpe 0.5, then the market variance should be $1/(1 + 3^2) = 1/10$ of the total variance. For a large portfolio, typically the aggregation of many PM portfolios, the portfolio Sharpe Ratio is higher; a Sharpe of 2 yields a ratio of 5.9% and of 3 a ratio of 2.7%.

- Your portfolio has an annualized dollar volatility, as a percentage of GMV, equal to σ_{port} and the market has an annualized percent volatility σ_m. The total variance is equal to the sum of the portfolio variance and of the market variance. The optimal percentage GMV allocated to the market is

$$\frac{GMV_m}{GMV_{total}} = \frac{1}{1 + \frac{\sigma_m \times (Sharpe\ Ratio)_{port}}{\sigma_{port} \times (Sharpe\ Ratio)_m}}$$

Let us consider a numerical example: $\sigma_{port} = 3\%$, $\sigma_m = 15\%$, Sharpe$_m = 0.5$, Sharpe$_w = 1.5$. The ratio is 6.25%.

If we consider a large portfolio, then σ_{port} is smaller.[9] For 1,000 stocks, and assuming percentage idio of a stock 20%, $\sigma_{port} = 0.6\%$. Assume Sharpe$_w = 2$. Then $GMV_m/GMV_{total} = 1\%$.

Summing up: a small independent PM maximizing Sharpe Ratio can have a small net exposure to the market. On the other side, a large portfolio composed of multiple portfolios managed by different PMs has higher Sharpe Ratio and lower volatility and should run essentially market-neutral. As a consequence the PMs contributing to this portfolio should run market neutral as well. In addition to considerations of Sharpe maximization, there are independent considerations related

---

[8] The proof of this is in the Appendix, 11.3.1.
[9] For a portfolio that has no factor risk and stocks with identical idio vol, the formula $\sigma_{port} = \sigma_{stock}/\sqrt{no.stocks}$ is a first approximation.

to the mandate of the fund. For example, if the fund promises returns uncorrelated to the market, the optimal vol and GMV allocated to the market is zero by necessity.

7.2.3   Setting an Upper Limit on Single-Stock Holdings

A portfolio, by definition, is composed by several assets. For a moment, let's pause and consider *why* we invest in many assets. There are, after all, commodity traders who invest in a limited number of assets. What should a fundamental investor be any different? Why not specialize in a single company? There are many possible reasons. There are limits to the knowledge of a single company, and being long and short a single asset may not be profitable enough. On the other side, companies in the same industries enjoy similarities, so that there are increasing returns to scale in covering and trading them as a group. Moreover, a diverse coverage enables a manager to compare their relative strengths and trade pairs or baskets. Perhaps the most important reason is *diversification*. Bets "average out". The risk of n independent bets is lower than the risk of any one bet. If conviction is identical across stocks, then the optimal sizing yields a diversified portfolio; this was the subject of Section 6.3. This is not the whole story, though. Imagine the case of a PM with an abnormal conviction in one stock. According to some sizing criterion followed by the PM, the position in the stock is 40% of the portfolio's GMV. Should this be allowed? Common sense suggests not, although there are hedge funds allowing this concentration level, or more. As is often the case, there are no wrong answers, only trade-offs. Upper limits on single stocks stem from two separate considerations. First, stocks are not infinitely liquid. In the course of a distressing event, you may want to reduce the size of your portfolio; in certain cases, you may *have* to cut to meet certain limits imposed by the fund administrator, like maximum volatility limits or stop-loss limits. In extreme cases, you may have to cut to meet prime broker margin requirements on your portfolio. Stock liquidity itself is not independent of distress conditions: it is lower when people need it the most. However, a first approximation of asset liquidity is its average daily trading volume (ADTV), expressed in dollars/day, usually measured over 30 days to six months. The liquidity of a position can then be measured in units of its ADTV; if a holding is

$20M, and its ADTC is $10M/day, then we say that the position is "2 day volume". In turn, this value tells us what is the expected number of days needed to liquidate the position: if we trade every day a maximum of, say, 4% of total trading volume, to trade out of a position will take 50 trading days. This horizon has to be contrasted with the investment horizon of the trader, and also with other constraints set by the risk manager. For example, if the fund's assets can be entirely redeemed at one month's notice, then a liquidation interval of 50 days is too long, and the investment manager will require a stricter per-stock liquidity limit, always expressed as a percentage of ADTV.

The second consideration is that portfolio managers are not gods, despite their best intentions.[10] Their theses are unprofitable in almost 50% of cases. The limit on a single position takes into account the low signal-to-noise ratio embedded in investment theses and teases the most out of it by forcing a large number of effective bets at any given time. Consider the extreme example of a trader whose only skill is to predict (imperfectly) whether each stock that he covers will have a positive or negative idiosyncratic return in the following month, but without any ability to predict the return magnitude. In this case, the right thing to do is to size equally all the positions in the portfolio. At the other extreme is a PM who, when he is right about the direction of the return, guesses the size of the return exactly. How should he size the positions? The answer to this question is not obvious. In order to be well-defined, it requires additional assumptions; however, we can imagine that the sizing will be, if not proportional to the expected return, certainly not uniform. One way to quantify the trade-off between concentration and sizing skill is to consider the minimum number of bets that can be placed in the portfolio. If the portfolio manager has an investment universe of 100 stocks, and a maximum single-stock limit of 20% of GMV, then the smallest number of stocks in the portfolio is 5. Let us denote α_h (for "high conviction") the realized average return in these high-conviction positions. Here we are considering idio returns, which are uncorrelated. Let's make another simplifying assumption: the stocks have all the same volatility σ. Then the volatility of the portfolio is $(GMV/5) \times \sqrt{5}\sigma$. The realized

---

[10] "Prometheus" originates from Ancient Greek *pro-manthano*, "[I] learn in advance". He is the Saint Protector of overconfident portfolio managers.

return is $GMV \times \alpha_h$. The Sharpe Ratio is the ratio of the two:

$$(\textit{Sharpe high conviction}) = \frac{GMV \times \alpha_h}{(GMV/\sqrt{5}) \times \sigma} = \sqrt{5} \times \frac{\alpha_h}{\sigma}$$

Compare now to the case where we impose a limit of 1% GMV, i.e., we enforce complete diversification. The realized return of such low-conviction stocks is lower: α_ℓ (for "low conviction") is lower than α_h. The same calculation as above gives a Sharpe Ratio

$$(\textit{Sharpe low conviction}) = \sqrt{100} \times \frac{\alpha_\ell}{\sigma}$$

The question is whether (*Sharpe high conviction*) > (*Sharpe low conviction*). This is the case only if $\alpha_h > \alpha_\ell \sqrt{100/5}$. Is our best ideas alpha four and a half times as good as the undifferentiated alpha? Then, a limit of 20% GMV is justified. We can generalize the formula a bit

$$\alpha_h > \alpha_\ell \sqrt{(\text{\# stocks in the universe})/(1/(\text{max percentage})}$$

Then breakeven value for the single-stock limit is

$$\text{max percentage} = \left(\frac{\alpha_h}{\alpha_\ell}\right)^2 \times \frac{1}{(\text{\# stocks in the portfolio})}$$

This is quite insightful: the larger the ratio between realized returns for high-conviction stocks and low-conviction ones, the more concentrated the portfolio can be. We call this the *Conviction Profitability Ratio* or CPR. The more stocks in the portfolio, the less concentrated the portfolio: you can put 50% of your capital in a 20-stock portfolio; in a 200-stock portfolio, maybe not. In Table 7.4 I report some values for some combinations of the parameters. The number of stocks in the universe is known, the Conviction Profitability Ratio much less so. However, you may be surprised to know that for most PM it is one *or less*, and that even the best PMs don't exceed 2. A 100-stock portfolio with a Conviction Profitability Ratio of 2 results in a 4% GMV limit. I would emphasize that the definitions of α_h and α_ℓ should rely on some empirical evidence. In its absence, portfolio managers often overestimate their sizing skills. We devote Section 8.2.1 to the measure of this important dimension of performance.

Table 7.4   Single-Stock Limit, based on coverage
breadth and ratio between returns for high- vs.
low-conviction stocks.

α_h/α_ℓ	# stocks	Max Size
1.0	50	2.0%
1.5	50	4.5%
2.0	50	8.0%
1.0	100	1.0%
1.5	100	2.2%
2.0	100	4.0%
1.0	150	0.7%
1.5	150	1.5%
2.0	150	2.7%

In this section we have employed limits on GMV. An alternative, but equivalent, approach, is to use dollars of idiosyncratic volatility, and to take into account the fact that the volatility of stocks varies across one portfolio manager's universe. While this is certainly possible, my view is that the benefits of a more complex approach are limited for two reasons. First, as we saw in Section 6.3, the naïve assumption that expected return of a position is proportional to idio volatility is not quite confirmed in practice. We would need to perform a more careful analysis. The second objection to developing a complex model is that the CPR is measurable but, for any PM, it has a wide range. This error band in turn drives the range of possible single-stock limits. There is no need to fine-tune the formula when there is such a dominant and irreducible source of uncertainty.

7.2.4   Setting an Upper Limit on Single-Factor Exposures

We have seen what a reasonable limit of factor risk should be in Section 7.2.1, and what a reasonable limit should be on market risk in Section 7.2.2, or any risk-premium carrying factor, if you believe in their existence. We have been silent about the remaining factors. We consider a few options.

• **Keep the Factor Exposures to Zero**. Like becoming vegan or running the New York marathon, this is a tempting option until you actually try it. Every factor exposure constraint reduces your degrees of freedom. With 15 style factors and 80 assets, you have effectively a portfolio of 65 assets. This is not too terrible, except for the fact that managing a portfolio would require solving a linear system of equations every time you want to add or change an investment idea. Moreover, if you did not take into account transaction costs, you would likely trade excessively. You can include transaction costs, but this would require using a portfolio optimizer. At this point, the cognitive cost of managing the portfolio has exceeded the benefits of reducing unwanted risk. Moreover, we have learned in Section 7.2.1 that the costs of holding a small amount of factor risk are tolerable. Which brings us to the next option.

- **Keep Factor Risk Within a Certain Range**. This seems all that is needed. It controls the volatility of unwanted returns, and it allows for a certain wiggle room for factor exposures to change without having to micro-manage them. There is a problem, however. Portfolio managers are not gods, but neither are risk managers or the risk model providers. You can ask a good model to describe an important aspect of reality, not the whole of it. Reality is not stationary, and factors don't have always the same distribution. You are playing a coin-tossing game in which a fair coin can be suddenly replaced by a biased one. Out of metaphor, the short interest factor that as of today has a volatility of 1% annualized, may experience a run-up of 1% *in a single week*. The volatilities predicted by the risk model occasionally break. When they break, they do so spectacularly. This does not mean that the risk model is useless. A good quantitative model shows a way out even when it fails. In this case the way out is to control exposures, and not risk, to protect the portfolio from extreme, unforeseeable returns.

- **Keep Factor Exposures Within a Certain Range**. We don't know when extreme returns occur but, for any factor, we can have an estimate of their size. First, by looking at their history. The largest drawdown is a starting point to model worst-case events. Risk tolerance also plays a role, together with expert judgment. Assume, for example, that a partial ban on shorts becomes permanent in certain countries; or that margin requirements become stricter. In this case, history becomes less relevant, and we may want to consider a slightly lenient worst-case. The output of this analysis is a subjective worst-case return estimate for a factor over a certain horizon; say, $r_{factworst} = -5\%$ over a month. Another input in the analysis is the maximum percent $r_{portloss}$ loss that is tolerable from this factor. Then, the dollar exposure limit b_{max} on the factor is such that $b_{max} \times r_{factworst} = GMV \times r_{portloss}$. Then, the upper bound on the percentage exposure is

$$\frac{b_{max}}{GMV} = \frac{r_{portloss}}{r_{factworst}}$$

This is a simple limit. It is static: it does not depend on the portfolio's predicted risk, or on the factor's volatility. It is stricter if we have low tolerance for losses, or if the factor has large extreme returns. It is never going to be binding for many factors. The reason is that, for factors that exhibit high volatility like the market factor, or certain industry factors, the bound on total factor risk kicks in and forces the exposures to be low. For other factors with low volatility and low extreme returns, the limit is high, because the denominator $r_{factworst}$ is small. Finally, there are a few factors with low predicted volatility but high tail risk. This cast of characters can change, depending on how you construct the model. Short Interest, Hedge Fund Ownership, Liquidity, and even some value factors can occasionally constraint your portfolio. I close this section with a statement not based on hard empirical data, but on witnessing a large number of episodes: discipline in maintaining these limits will be well rewarded.

7.3   Systematic Hedging and Portfolio Management

There are scenarios in which the manual management of a portfolio becomes unwieldy. A few of them are listed below:

- You have a large number of analysts, covering either different subsets of stocks in your sector or, if you are a multi-sector portfolio manager, covering different sectors. Each analyst has trading authority and is in effect an autonomous portfolio manager. In this case, because of decentralized decisions, it is possible that the aggregation of these independent position blocks will result in high factor exposures. In addition to this, if the coverages of the analysts overlap, there is also the possibility that some positions may be too concentrated.

- If you have a centralized portfolio, but a large number of stocks, then adjusting factor exposures by trading only a handful of stocks with high marginal contribution to factor risk is inefficient. You may be better off trading a large number of stocks, but in smaller amounts, to reduce transaction costs and take into account simultaneous exposures to other factors.
- If your portfolio has a large GMV or volatility, then execution costs and the absolute size of positions become primary concerns. Most hedge funds impose an ownership limit of a stock (expressed as a percentage of the market capitalization of the stock) for disclosure and regulatory purposes; managing to these limits *and* to single-stock limits *and* to factor exposures is certainly possible, but it becomes a chore unto itself, taking several hours per week. On the other side, ignoring these guidelines, especially when you manage a big portfolio with a chance of a large dollar drawdown, is unwise.
- If you are managing a multi-PM hedge fund, then you will face a combination of these issues at the same time. You may still decide to maintain a strict autonomy among PMs, essentially managing the platform as a fund of funds. The hidden cost in this choice is the opportunity cost of not adopting more advanced techniques to simplify the life of your portfolio managers and maximizing the profitability of your fund.

We propose three approaches that reduce the effort required to manage the portfolio. The first one consists of running an *automatic hedging program*. In practice, this means that an optimization is run at regular intervals (typically daily). The optimization aims to minimize transaction costs, while bringing the portfolio factor exposure, factor risk, and single-factor exposures within limits, without affecting the original stock sizes chosen by the portfolio manager. The tradeable universe used in this optimization problem does not include only the stocks in the PM's coverage or in the PM's sector, but all stocks that are sufficiently liquid to be traded. Trading a larger stocks base allows the optimization to reduce transaction costs and obtain better hedges. Even if the problem is relatively straightforward, the quantitative formulation has some subtleties, which are discussed in Section 11.8.

The second approach consists of making *factor-mimicking portfolios*.[11] You can think of these portfolios as synthetic assets "mimicking" factor returns, i.e., reproducing them as accurately as possible. As a PM, you do not have to trade single stock any longer; but rather can access an internal facility that will produce "factors on demand". Reducing factor risk is as simple as trading a well-crafted factor ETF. The core positions of the portfolio are not affected at all by the factor-mimicking portfolios.

The third approach is a *fully automated portfolio construction*. In this construct, the PM only inputs investment ideas, and the portfolio optimizer generates a portfolio that is (a) traded efficiently; (b) reflects the core ideas of the analysts in the sizing of the positions; (c) has its factor risk within limits. You can think of it as systematic single-portfolio optimization; the portfolio's positions are updated when new ideas come in; when the market conditions change (i.e., when loadings and volatilities change); or when both events occur.

Summing up, when it comes to ongoing portfolio management, we have seen at least five ways to go about it. In approximate order of complexity, they are

1. *Marginal risk-reducing trades*;
2. *Single-portfolio optimization*;
3. *Systematic factor hedging*;
4. *Trading factor portfolios*;
5. *Fully automated portfolio management.*

Which one you should adopt depends on the following considerations:

- Complexity of your portfolio. Higher number of stocks and of analysts warrants more sophisticated approaches.
- Level of comfort and trust in quantitative methods. A way to think about these methods is as if they were self-driving technology, but

---

[11] These portfolios are introduced in Section 4.3, and defined in Section 11.2.

for investing. The same self-driving car can be perceived by different drivers as liberating ("I can read a book") or disempowering ("I don't trust the car, and I *enjoy* driving!"). Quantitative methods should not be foisted on investors, but rather adopted gradually, tested and embraced by them.

- Resources to implement them. Marginal risk-reducing trades can be implemented in a spreadsheet; single-portfolio optimization is available in commercial software with GUIs for portfolio managers; the last three solutions require dedicated quantitative research with specific expertise.
- Capital utilization. Generating factor-mimicking portfolios consumes more capital, and so does systematic hedging using a broad universe of stocks. Empirically, the increased capital utilization is often not a determining issue, and it is more than compensated by the lower trading costs and better hedging performance; but it should not be ignored in the design phase.

7.4 Takeaway Messages

1. Generate your convictions using fundamental research.
2. Turn them into positions using a proportional of vol scaling rule.
3. Measure portfolio risk decomposition, and update your portfolio keeping in mind factor risk.
4. There are five levels of day-to-day portfolio management:
   a. *Marginal risk-reducing trades;*
   b. *Single-portfolio optimization;*
   c. *Systematic factor hedging;*
   d. *Trading factor portfolios;*
   e. *Fully automated portfolio management.*
5. For *marginal risk-reducing trades*, perform the following:
   a. Add/update an idea in the portfolio *pro-forma*.
   b. Check the change in %idio var.
   c. If there is a sizable change, identify the source(s) of factor risk, e.g., industry, country, style.

(continued)

(Continued)

    d. Identify the stocks that are largest marginal contributors to risk and update their position, compatibly with your fundamental conviction.

6. Regarding *risk limits*:

    a. Set risk limits on %idio, style and factor variance that are compatible with your investment style, and operate within them.

    b. Don't go below 70% idio var, and almost never below 50%.

    c. Keep a single-position GMV limit, increasing in your ability to select high-conviction names, and decreasing in the number of stocks in your portfolio.

    d. Keep a single-factor exposure limit, based on your loss tolerance and the worst-case factor returns.

7. When you need higher productivity and can afford more advanced tools, consider implementing an automated hedging program. This will generate perfect hedges that you can choose to include in your portfolio.

Chapter 8

Understand Your Performance

- *What will you learn here:* How to understand your realized performance. What you are good at, and what you can improve upon.
- *Why do you need it:* No unexamined portfolio is worth investing. In order to become a better portfolio manager, you want to understand how much of your past performance is due to luck vs. skill (factor PnL vs. idiosyncratic PnL), and how selection, sizing and timing contribute to your performance.
- *When will you need this:* On a monthly or quarterly basis.

8.1   Factor

The Earth rotates around the Sun at a speed of 67,000mph. When I go out for my occasional run, my own speed is in the tens of thousands of miles per hour. Should I take credit for this amazing performance? I wouldn't be completely lying if I bragged about this with friends (which I do); but it would be more transparent if I mentioned that my speed record is in *the frame reference of the Sun*. In this frame of reference, my speed is indistinguishable from Usain Bolt's. This factoid obscures the vast difference in skill between the two of us. To really understand the difference, *we need to change the frame of reference*. Another way to interpret the decomposition of returns is a method to change the frame of reference in investing. Total returns – and a portfolio's total PnL – live in the Sun's frame of reference. It is easy to fool ourselves with the belief that we beat birds, airplanes and supermen at their own game. Idiosyncratic returns and PnL live in the Earth's frame of reference. If we want to compare our performance to that of our peers, or to our very own past performance, we need to move to this frame. Factor-based performance attribution makes it possible.

8.1.1   *Performance Attribution*

We have met simple performance attribution before, for example, in Section 3.4.2. A more general attribution follows from Equation (7.1), which we reproduce here with a small change: we compute the *total* performance attribution during a time interval:

$$\text{total PnL}(T) = \sum_{t=1}^{T} \text{idio PnL}(t) + \text{factor PnL}(t)$$

and the factor PnL can be split in the PnL of the individual factors:

$$\text{factor PnL}(t) = \sum_{t=1}^{T} [\text{factor PnL}_1(t) + \text{factor PnL}_2(t) + \ldots]$$

This shows that the time series of the PnL of a strategy is the sum of an idio and a factor series. The factor PnL can be split in to subgroups like country, industry, and style.

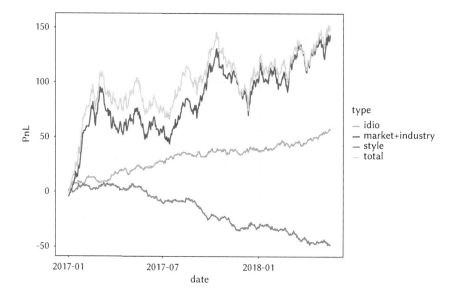

Figure 8.1   Performance Attribution example. The figure shows total PnL, idio PnL, market and industry PnL grouped together, and style PnL grouped together.

Consider a concrete example of a PM running a US net-long portfolio (400 long by 100 short). In Figure 8.1 we show the total PnL and its components: country[1] + industry factor PnL, style factor PnL, and idio PnL. The Total PnL has a Sharpe Ratio of 1.56. This may be interpreted as a sign of skill, but it is of course mainly attributable to the market, something that could be noted from the time-series attribution of the strategy. Although not many strategies report their time-series performance attribution, they do report their "beta" and their under/outperformance to the benchmark. However, if we only look at the total PnL net of market and industry, we are missing a deeper truth. Consider Figure 8.2. The returns net of market are now mediocre. The idiosyncratic PnL, however, is excellent, with a Sharpe Ratio of 2.4. The Style PnL nullifies the gains in idiosyncratic PnL. This is good news. Style PnL is not destiny; a recurring theme in this book is that factor risk and PnL can be managed. To this effect, let us go one level down. In Figure 8.3 we can see that the cause of the PnL

---

[1] "Country" may be replaced by "market" for single-country models.

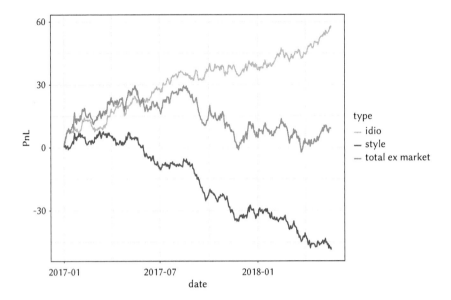

Figure 8.2 Performance Attribution example. The figure shows total PnL ex market PnL, idio PnL, and style PnL.

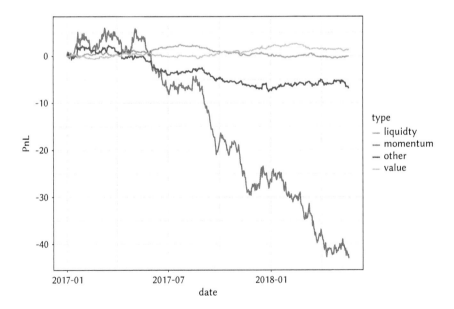

Figure 8.3 Performance Attribution example. The figure shows some of the largest contributors to style PnL.

Table 8.1 Portfolio Factor exposures.

Factor	Exposure ($M)	%Factor Variance
Momentum	124	30
Value	−15	9
Liquidity	48	7.3
...	...	...

is momentum. The average factor exposures and percentage variance of the portfolio are shown in Table 8.1, and they confirm that momentum exposure has been positive in the period under consideration and that momentum has been responsible for a large percentage of factor variance.

8.2   Idiosyncratic

If managing factor risk well was sufficient to be a great fundamental investor, I'd be managing a portfolio right now, not writing this book. The simple fact is that factors can find infinite ways to mar your performance, but cannot tell you how to be profitable. To make further progress, we need to understand idiosyncratic performance. You may ask: *What, exactly, is there to understand?* Isn't this the product of our insight, generating beautiful uncorrelated returns with the rest of the universe? Even the single-stock idio PnLs in a portfolio are uncorrelated from each other. To this sensible question I can only answer that *things are not as simple as they seem*. We will look into several innocent-looking questions:

- Even if stock idiosyncratic returns are uncorrelated, there is the non-negligible aspect that you are taking different levels of risk in each one of them. We discussed sizing already in Section 6.3. There, we assumed that our alphas are reliable. Here, we analyze the realized performance of our portfolio to determine whether we have any skill in sizing.
- It is convenient to think of portfolios as a sequence of static objects: here is my portfolio today and its daily PnL; tomorrow is another day. However, portfolios live in time, and the investment ideas that

they embody change slowly every day. It is important to understand how ideas decay over time.

- Combining the previous two points, we decompose performance into three components: selection, sizing and timing. These three dimensions are a powerful summary of our investment style and edge.
- Finally, we touch upon the topic of portfolio diversification, and its relationship with hit rate.

8.2.1 Selection, Sizing, Timing

The goal of this section is to decompose idiosyncratic PnL into interpretable terms:

$$PnL(Idio) = (selection\ PnL) + (sizing\ PnL) + (timing\ PnL)$$

Selection is about being directionally right; sizing is about being right about the absolute value of returns; timing is about taking on portfolio risk at the right time, i.e., when your theses are more correct than average. We start with selection and sizing.

Stock Selection and Stock Sizing. Your historical strategy is a list of dates, tickers and net market values. The net market value is the end-of-day value for a ticker on a given date. As a toy example, we consider a handful of tickers over two days, as shown in Table 8.2. However, it is easier to interpret and modify the strategy if it is represented in a "wide" tabular format, as shown in Table 8.3. Here, the dates are columns, the assets are rows, and value in the array is the closing net market value on a date, for an asset.

The reason for this rearrangement is that it makes it easier to reason about our investment choices. We can perform a "what-if" analysis by changing the values in our past allocation, and then compute the impact on performance. A natural transformation is to make the *size* of the investment equal within each date while keeping the *side* unchanged. CVX was a $137M long, which is over-size within the portfolio: we reduce it so that it is equal in GMV to WMB, which was a mere $6M short. We make the equalization so that the GMV of the entire portfolio is unchanged on 1/4/2018. We repeat the procedure for date 1/5/2018. The result is shown in Table 8.4. We now have a different strategy, termed *cross-sectional-equalized* (XSE), one in which we

Table 8.2 A list of position/dates/NMV.

Date	Ticker	NMV ($M)
2018-01-04	CVX	137
2018-01-04	MRO	−75
2018-01-04	OXY	−12
2018-01-04	WMB	11
2018-01-04	XOM	52
2018-01-05	CVX	−122
2018-01-05	MRO	−176
2018-01-05	OXY	−64
2018-01-05	WMB	−40
2018-01-05	XOM	51

Table 8.3 A list of position/dates/NMV, rearranged in matrix form.

Ticker	2018-01-04	2018-01-05
CVX	137	−122
MRO	−75	176
OXY	−12	−64
WMB	−6	−40
XOM	−42	51

Table 8.4 A list of position / dates / nmv, rearranged in matrix form with equalized net market values within each date.

Ticker	2018-01-04	2018-01-05
CVX	54.4	−90.6
MRO	−54.4	90.6
OXY	−54.4	−90.6
WMB	−54.4	−90.6
XOM	−54.4	90.6

have removed sizing from the equation. We can compute the PnL and the Sharpe Ratio of this equal-sized strategy over, say, the course of 2018. Before we delve into it, there are a few things to keep in mind:

1. We should not consider all the positions in the portfolio. Some NMVs are likely to be very small and the positions not economically important. These can be instances of stocks that are being liquidated; stocks that are illiquid and that we are reluctant to trade; and finally, stock we may just have forgotten about (not a commendable habit!). In any event, we should set a minimum GMV threshold, based on judgment and economic significance. A threshold of $1M in a portfolio with 70–80 names with a GMV of $500M–1B seems sensible; but ultimately it is up to you to decide what minimum GMV represents a conscious investment decision.

2. We should analyze only the idiosyncratic performance. An equal-sized portfolio is not built with factor risk in mind, and that is fine. One of the great advantages of factor modeling is the *separation of concerns*: we can focus on idio PnL first and see whether we are any good at it. Say our equal-sized portfolio is performing well. Then we can build a portfolio that is not too different from the equal-sized portfolio and yet has small factor risk.

3. We are ignoring transaction costs. Sometimes, the small positions in the original strategy are not the result of investment conviction but rather stem from the material impossibility to express our ideas in the portfolio. For example, our intent was to own $40M of WMB, but it trades $20M/day, which is much less than other energy companies in the portfolio. A $55M position in WMB is unrealistic. We will address this in later stages of the analysis. For the time being, let us keep this in mind.

4. For portfolios, we may want to convert the size of the portfolio from GMV to idio dollar volatility; i.e., we resize the portfolio positions so that they have all the same dollar idio vol, and that the portfolio dollar idio vol is the same as the original portfolio.

The last two items in the list above are more demanding to implement, but not so hard that they cannot be set up in an excel spreadsheet, once a commercial risk model is available.

Portfolio	Type	Sharpe Ratio
long	raw portfolio	2.9
long	equal-sized portfolio	3.4
long & short	raw portfolio	3.2
long & short	equal-sized portfolio	3.4
short	raw portfolio	1.9
short	equal-sized portfolio	1.5

The results of this simulation are shown in the top panel of Figure 8.4. From the charts and the table we can see that the performance of the overall book benefits from more equal sizing. The return is actually lower for the equal-sized book vs. actual book, but the Sharpe Ratio is slightly higher. A lower return for the long/short book should hardly come as a surprise. The equal-sized portfolio is more diversified and therefore has lower volatility; however, *a higher Sharpe means that we can scale up the GMV and with the same risk budget, achieve a higher PnL* (as discussed in Section 6.1 and Chapter 10). There are additional insights in these figures. The long side of the book has much higher Sharpe Ratio when it is equal sized, whereas the historical short side of the book has much higher Sharpe Ratio than the equal-sized one. A natural question in a case like this is: Why is this happening? Perhaps the PM has a replicable skill in identifying shorts; or, alternatively, the answer could have been that there were a few great shorting opportunities that will never present themselves again. And finally, the luck explanation: the crash of a stock due to the litigation that no one had foreseen; the acquisition offer that was not received favorably by the market; the accounting scandal. A way to identify the large relative winners and losers is via a heatmap graph, as shown in the bottom panel of Figure 8.4. A blue square tells you that the equal-sized portfolio would have outperformed for that particular stock. The point I want to convey here is that quantitative analysis is helpful in itself, but it is most helpful when it is combined with detailed, qualitative knowledge. The answer to these questions will determine how the PM should size the long and the short ideas in the portfolio. If we take these numbers at face value (and again, we shouldn't!), a possible scenario could be:

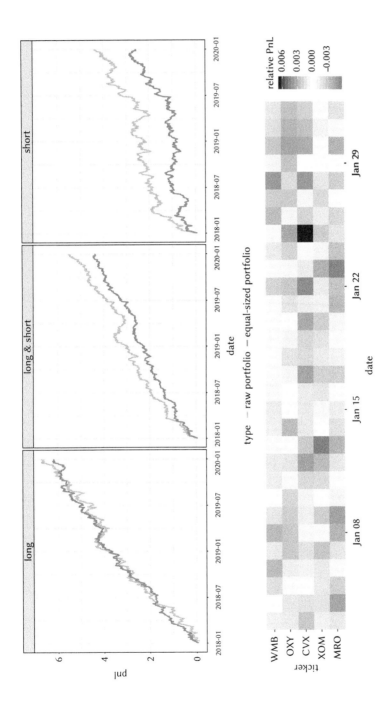

Figure 8.4 Top: Idiosyncratic performance of equal-sized vs. actual-sized portfolios. Short and Long sizes are shown separately. Middle: The relative performance of individual stocks over time in the portfolio. Bottom: Risk-adjusted performance of a portfolio vs. equal-sized portfolio, aggregate long & short, and by side.

132

(a) make your longs more uniform and increase the GMV of the long book; (b) maintain your sizing in shorts; (c) potentially add a short SPX future to counterbalance the increased long positions, and adjust the shorts to reduce exposures to other factors.

The importance of liquidity. Understanding one's sizing skill is very important, and there is even some deep mathematics in it, which is beyond the scope of this book. However, there is one major issue we have not addressed: liquidity constraints. This was the third item in our list of caveats and it can invalidate the entire analysis if the strategy has a large gross market value, or if its profitability depends on trading events. Certain portfolios can run several billions of GMV with as few as 50 assets. In this case, building a single position, even in a very liquid name, can take months, and simulating a fully built position from day one will result in very different, and unrealistic, PnL from what can be achieved. But the portfolio need not be very large for the sizing/hitting decomposition alone to be inadequate. A significant percentage of the PnL of a fundamental equity portfolio is realized around earnings, i.e., between the day prior to announcement and the day after. The position cannot, and should not, be built quickly, because transaction costs would nullify the alpha in the stock. We devote a section to rules of thumb for this very problem. If that is the case, assuming equal sizes is unrealistic and incorrect. Should we throw away all the beautiful charts I generated for this section? Luckily, no, on two accounts. First, the idealized analysis is still useful. It shows the selection and sizing skill of a PM when the portfolio size is in itself not a concern. If these skills are there *pro forma* in a paper portfolio, but are not realized in the dollar portfolio, then we can be assured that this has to do with the deployment of the strategy – maybe its capacity is lower than we thought – or with the execution of the strategy itself; for example, participation rate may be too high, and thus performance could be eroded by execution costs.

The second reason not to despair is that there is a way to refine this analysis. The refinement includes the procedure we presented so far as a special case when there are no transaction costs. The idea is simple. We preserve the concept of equal-sized positions; however, we add the constraint that on each day, we cannot trade for each stock more than a given percentage of the daily volume of the stock. This is a realistic constraint; well-managed funds impose such a constraint

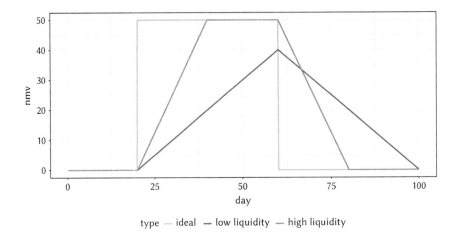

Figure 8.5   Liquidity-constrained simulation.

on PM trading behavior to keep their transaction costs in check; moreover, trading at a certain fixed participation rate is the best practice.
Figure 8.5 shows the impact of a liquidity constraint on trading. The
red line corresponds to lack of transaction costs to achieve a target
NMV of $50M. If we have a max trading limit of $2.5M/day, then it will
take 20 days to build the position up to the target, and 20 to unwind
it; this is the blue line. If the stock is more illiquid and we can trade
only $1M/day, then, by the time we have changed our fundamental
view about the stock, we have not fully built the position yet; this is
the green line. Simulating this portfolio requires some more work. A
description of the optimization formulation and of the procedure is in
Section 11.6.1.

  Timing. Intuitively, having "timing" skill means to be able to
profit from a stock's returns not because it has a positive (or negative)
expected return but because we are on the right side of the stock,
both when it has positive *and* negative returns. Identifying trends
in a stock's return is a long-term, strategic skill; timing a stock's
return is inherently a short-term, tactical skill. By her very nature,
a fundamental investor is a strategic thinker. It should not come
as a surprise that "timing" is hard, and that most investors don't
possess this skill. Nevertheless, understanding timing is as important

Table 8.5   A list of position/date/nmv, rearranged in matrix form.

Ticker	2018-01-04	2018-01-05
CVX	73	−73
MRO	−73	73
OXY	−73	−73
WMB	−73	−73
XOM	−73	73

as understanding sizing, at the very least, because having *negative* timing skills can be remedied, similarly to having negative sizing skills. In addition, monitoring timing over time (I know, lame pun) is useful. Are we getting better? Worse? Are our ideas lasting longer? And, most importantly, how can we take action to increase the profitability of our strategy?

The core idea behind sizing analysis was to compare the performance of the live portfolio to that of a portfolio in which sizing information was eliminated for each date. We generalize this approach, and equalize non-zero positions for each stock *and* across all dates. In Table 8.5 I go back to our toy portfolio example: the positions are equal-sized across assets and time. We could then compute the performance of the equalized strategy. The cross-sectional time-size-equalized (XSTSE) strategy differs from the XSE strategy in one aspect only: in XSTSE, the GMV is identical across dates, in XSE it can differ.

Some notes:

- The GMV is constant if the number of fundamental ideas doesn't change over time. To a first approximation this is appropriate; and when the number of ideas do change over time, then assuming that the GMV scales with the number of ideas makes intuitive sense.
- As we did for the sizing analysis, we can do constant volatility targeting instead of constant GMV targeting. When performing GMV targeting, we care about returns; when performing volatility targeting, we care about Sharpe.
- As we did for the sizing analysis, we can perform a liquidity-aware timing skill analysis.

In summary, we can decompose the PnL of an actual strategy by subtracting and summing the PnL of simpler and simpler strategies:

$$\text{PnL(Idio)} = [\text{PnL(Idio)} - \text{PnL(XSE)}]+$$
$$[\text{PnL(XSE)} - \text{PnL(XSTSE)}]+$$
$$\text{PnL(XSTSE)}$$
$$= (sizing\ PnL)+$$
$$(timing\ PnL)+$$
$$(selection\ PnL)$$

There is anecdotal evidence that PMs have at best very little timing skill, moderately-positive-to-moderately-negative sizing skill, and primarily selection skills. When you detect positive sizing or timing skill, you should treasure it and nurture it. When you don't, you can improve your performance by equalizing your positions within each date and/or across time.

8.2.2   The Relationship Between Performance and Diversification

Diversification is not a skill. You can plan for it, add more stocks to your portfolio over time. It does not come for free, but its blessings are many, and every portfolio manager must count and understand them.

Say that an investor's portfolio has a certain probability of guessing the right side of stock returns across dates and assets. You can estimate this by taking the number dates-asset pairs with either positive idiosyncratic returns and long positions (hence yielding a positive PnL) or negative idiosyncratic returns and short positions, divided by all date-asset pairs instances in a strategy. This probability is in general greater than 50%, but not by much. I show in the appendix that the Information Ratio takes the form

$$(Inf.Ratio) = [2 \times (hitting\ probability) - 1] \times$$
$$\sqrt{252 \times (effective\ number\ of\ stocks)}$$

The *effective number of stocks* in the portfolio is equal to the actual number of stocks in the portfolio if the positions are identical, but it is smaller than that if the positions are concentrated. The exact formula is given by Procedure[2] 8.1: for simplicity, we keep to the case where we have identical positions. The formula highlights two phenomena. First, that diversification is good for risk-adjusted performance. PnL sums up, but PnL fluctuations average out. A second fact becomes obvious when we consider a few numerical examples: you don't need a high hitting probability to have great performance. Say that hitting probability is 51% and the portfolio has a size of 70 stocks. Then the Information Ratio is $(2 \times 0.51 - 1) \times \sqrt{252 \times 70} = 2.6$. This is an excellent IR. In fact, even a hitting probability $= 50.5\%$ gives an IR of 1.3. The formula also explains why statistical arbitrage strategies can achieve such high risk-adjusted performances. The number of stocks is in the thousands; if $N_e = 3000$, to achieve an IR of 8, it is sufficient to have a hitting probability of 50.5%. The power of diversification is great. It is not a skill: it is a *skill multiplier*. What is not to like about it? One should take the portfolio breadth to the proverbial 11 (or 11,000). The next paragraph should bring the message home: diversification is central but is not a panacea for fundamental investors. The reason is that we assumed that hitting probabilities are a constant by Portfolio Manager, independent of the breadth of coverage. This is not true. Beyond a certain threshold, coverage and breadth increase at the expense of accuracy. This occurs whether the PM expands her coverage, or whether she hires additional PMs to cover additional stocks, because in either case the overhead needed to coordinate the effort of the team is at the expense of the time budget used to analyze companies. Finding the optimal breadth, where marginal costs equal marginal benefit, is not straightforward. Year-over-year performance comparisons are confounded by the large variation in hitting probability during the same time interval. We can experience higher Information Ratio *and* smaller breadth! Let us give an example. After the initial ramp-up of a strategy to an effective number of positions of 80 assets, a PM experiences a Sharpe Ratio of 1.4. This corresponds to a hitting probability of 50.5%. On the

---

[2] For a derivation, see the Appendix 11.2.

following year, she gradually increases coverage over a year to 100; the effective number of positions, averaged during the course of the year, is 90. The increase in Information Ratio, if hitting rate stays constant, would be equal to $\sqrt{90/80} = 1.06$; i.e., a change of about 6%. If the true hitting rate is 50.5%, the measured hitting rate is not always 50.5%, because we only observe a finite number of date/asset returns. If, considering the most extreme scenario, we observed only one event, the probability would be either 0 or 1! The standard error[3] associated to this yearly hitting rate is 0.33%. This is a very large value, comparable to the "edge" of 0.5%. In fact, the probability that, because of these fluctuations, the PM will observe a lower Information Ratio even after having increased her breadth, is very high, only slightly less than 50%. This does not imply that breadth increase is not useful. Increasing coverage from 5 to 50 names is extremely useful; increasing it from 50 to 70 is also useful in the long run, since it yields an IR increase of almost 20%. If the increase occurs by adding analysts covering the additional 20 stocks, there is no trade-off (provided that the analyst has a hit rate similar to the PM, of course); if the increase occurs by splitting the PM's time among more stocks, the benefit is not as clear-cut. To paraphrase Einstein, the takeaway here is *increase diversification as much as you can, but not more.*

Procedure 8.1 Effective number of stocks in a portfolio.

- For each stock in the portfolio, compute the percentage of the total GMV invested in this stock.
- Compute the sum of the squares of these quantities:

$$H = \text{sum}[\%GMV^2(\text{stock } i)]$$

- The *effective number of stocks* is

$$(\text{effective number of stocks}) = 1/H$$

---

[3] This is equal to $\sqrt{0.505 \times (1 - 0.505)/(90 \times 252)} = 0.33\%$.

> **Insight 8.1** Diversification benefits.
>
> Having a broader portfolio is beneficial to risk-adjusted perfor-
> mance in proportion to the square root of the effective number
> of stocks, provided that the ability to forecast returns at the asset
> level is not negatively impacted.

8.3   Trade Events Efficiently

The majority of this book deals with portfolio construction in light
of fundamental convictions about the mispricing of an asset. As a
portfolio manager, you update your beliefs and modify the portfolio accordingly. The value of a company is not usually related to the
occurrence of an event scheduled in advance. This is different from
other investing styles and classes where expressing views on future
events is central to a strategy. Macro investing, risk arbitrage and index
arbitrage, for example, rely on informed views on events. Even fundamental investing, however, has a place for event trading. Earnings
announcements constitute an important source of profit for portfolio
managers. The share of PnL attributable to returns around earnings
varies by sector and by years: financial stocks are less sensitive to
earnings announcements than biotech and pharma; and in years in
which market volatility is low, impact of earnings is proportionally
higher. In all cases, indicatively a PM can receive anywhere between
25% and 50% of her PnL from earnings-related bets. For this reason, it
is important to develop a rational process for positioning and trading
around earnings, or at least, to think systematically about the issue.

We consider the simplest case. You, the PM, have developed a thesis
regarding the expected return of a stock on earnings date. You expect
a 4% return on that day, which is two weeks away. A few questions:

1. How big should the position be?
2. Should we take into account the risk contribution when sizing the
   position?

3. How should we trade into the event?
4. How do transaction costs enter the picture?

Some simple heuristics that seem common knowledge are the following:

1. Size at the event should be proportional to expected return;
2. Size at the event should be smaller if, everything else being equal, transaction costs are higher;
3. If the time from thesis formation to the event is shorter, everything else being equal, the size at the event should be smaller because there is less time to build it;
4. Following the event, the position should be exited, as it consumes the risk and capital budget of the PM.

These are sensible rules, but are they based in evidence? And can we formulate some rough quantitative prescription on sizing and trading strategy? The strategy here is to (a) formulate a very simple model, which will (b) confirm the heuristic rules we just formulated and (c) provide simple quantitative estimates useful in real life.

There are building blocks needed to build a successful trade. The first one is the return on the effective date, and it's an easy one to reason about: the expected PnL from this term is simply proportional to the position's size on event date. The second block is the transaction cost from trading. Commissions and the bid–ask spread are a small fraction of this cost; *market impact* is the dominant contributor to transaction costs, when trading for events and otherwise. To understand market impact, think of a stock price as a spring. When you participate in a trade, you pull this spring. When you are done trading, the price goes back to equilibrium, but you don't receive credit for the effort of pulling it in the first place. Out of metaphor, any trade moves the price, if only by a small amount. As you keep trading in the same direction in order to complete the order, the price you pay is the one that was affected by your trading so far. When the trade is complete, the average price you paid is higher than the initial price at the start of the trade. The stock price "relaxes" back to its original value. In real life, this sequence of events is masked by noise, and it is difficult to discern it in a single trade. Over many trades, however, it is a very robust finding, and you are better off not ignoring it. Are there formulas for the market impact? Everything else being equal, i.e., for a given stock, over a fixed trading horizon, there is plenty of empirical evidence that the cost increases faster than linearly in the dollar amount traded, specifically between $\sqrt{(trade\ size)^3}$ and $(trade\ size)^2$. The volatility of the stock and its trading volume play a role, too. More volatile stocks have a larger market impact; so do less traded stocks. Based on this information alone, let us attempt a rule-of-thumb to guess the best trading size for an event.

Say that we trade at a constant percentage of volume from now to the event date, and after the event we liquidate at the same rate. We want to find the trading size that maximizes the PnL net of transaction costs. If we use the quadratic impact model, then the problem is

$$maximize\ (expected\ return) \times (trade\ size) - \frac{constant}{2} \times (trade\ size)^2$$

The solution to this problem is that we should trade in proportion to the constant factor. Let's skip all the details, and go directly to a formula that employs the stock parameters you know about: its daily volatility σ, its daily dollar volume V, and the time until the event T. If the expected return is denoted by α, the optimal trade size is given by

$$(optimal\ trade\ size) = C \times \frac{\alpha \times V \times T}{2\sigma}$$

The value of C is specific to the market but is independent of the stock.[4] You will need to have access to a market impact model estimated on recent data to have an estimate of C. The sizing formula is simple, but leaves several questions unanswered. The first one, quite naturally, is whether the modeling assumptions are realistic. The second question concerns the implications for systematic risk, which we have so far ignored. The third question: What about liquidating the stock after the event? The back-of-the-envelope calculation is silent on it.

Answering these questions is not easy. If we take as a starting point quadratic t-costs, and the common variance risk penalty, then we can work out the optimal course of action. Here are the major points:

---

[4] For a derivation of this formula, see Section 11.9 and Equation (11.9). The detailed model is more general, and could be of use to PMs whose PnL is driven by a few large calendar events.

- Trading at constant participation rate of the stock's trading volume (VWAP) is optimal. Check that single-position concentration is not excessive. Around earnings, you will probably temporarily breach risk limits. This is one occasion in which you consider whether the breach is short enough to grant yourself an override.
- If you hold a concentrated portfolio, or are trading a few large events, then risk considerations are very important. The heuristic no longer works well. The optimal trade size at event is a "discounted" version of the heuristic, where the discount depends on the risk penalty. And trading should not occur at constant rate but at an *increasing* rate going into the event; and liquidation should likewise be faster after the event. The reason for this modification is that you don't want to hold the risk accumulated early in the trade for its entire duration.

The last bullet point hints at the increased complexity of the problem when the trade is large. Should you find yourself in this situation, the Appendix provides a starting point, which needs to be complemented by a healthy amount of simulations and customization to your specific instance.

8.4   ★Use Alternative Data!

The availability of new data sources is one of the large and persistent trends in business and finance of the past two decades. The slogan "Data is the new oil" has some truth to it. It is abundant if one has right technology to extract it; it can be transformed in countless new products, and these products create and destroy entire industries. In finance specifically, new data sets that are large (think terabytes to exabytes), alternative in nature (think transactional data or satellite images) and unstructured (text, images) are becoming available every day. There are dedicated financial providers (for a survey of these providers, Kolanovic and Krishnamachari [2017] and its updated editions is a good reference); conferences like BattleFin showcase the latest products; banks have their own proprietary offerings. They have been adopted first by quantitative strategies, and more recently by fundamental ones. There is no agreed-upon framework for the ingestion and usage of these data. Aside from the technical challenges of ingesting, storing and processing these data, here are some of the challenges that the PM faces:

1. If Big Data is the answer, what are the questions? What can you use these data for? Alpha? Risk? Tail Risk?
2. How do you display and consume the data? What are usable summaries of the data?
3. How do you tell whether a new piece of data is useful? All data vendors promise great value added (always in hindsight).
4. How do you integrate the data with your fundamental process?

These are open-ended, difficult questions, and the honest answer to most of them is "We don't know yet". Bradley Efron, one of the innovators of contemporary Statistics and Machine Learning, summarizes our state of affairs this way in his talk "The Future of Statistics":

- *19th Century: Large data sets, simple questions*
- *20th Century: Small data sets, simple questions*
- *21st Century: Large data sets, complex questions*

"Complex questions" in finance go beyond alpha and risk. *End-to-end learning* envisions the investment process as "data in, strategy out" with, in the middle, automated risk estimation, transaction cost estimation, alpha generation and portfolio optimization [Buehler et al., 2019].

We are a long way from realizing this vision. In the meantime, we can at least try to take advantage of an existing factor model framework to partially answer them. In order:

1. Alternative Data are useful primarily for alpha research, past performance attribution, and, secondarily, for risk prediction.
2. We compress the information into single-stock characteristics, similarly to factor loadings. Displaying characteristics per stock, and the exposure of the portfolio to these alternative data is analogous to factor models.
3. We evaluate the usefulness of the additional characteristics by estimating their power to predict the residual returns of the model, i.e., the return component that has not been explained by risk factors.
4. If the predictive power is sufficiently high, then the characteristics are incorporated in the investment process.

This does not come for free. To succeed, cooperation between data scientist and investment analyst is essential. The data scientist contributes technological and statistical know-how, while the investment analyst provides essential domain knowledge and more specifically in the following two sub-processes. First, raw data must be screened for their potential contributions to performance metrics that the PM considers relevant. In a few cases, the decision is trivial: for internet merchants in developed markets, the number of quarterly orders or the number and size of credit card transactions are tracking revenues fairly well. In other cases, the data are a piece of a wider puzzle. For example, say that, through a FOIA request, the data scientist can infer government procurement data with large industrial companies. This is useful information to estimate revenues, but it must be combined with preexisting estimates for non-government entities. Secondly, raw data must be converted into meaningful features. In some cases, z-scored levels matter (many factors in risk models are defined this way); in others, linear or multiplicative growth rates are more informative. The number of transformations is large, and I list a few of them in Appendix 11.5. And even more important, *composition* of information matters: some data are only sector-, industry- or country-specific. There are so many choices that generating all possible features from alternative data would be a recipe for confusion and data mining. In addition to the proviso that there is no free lunch when using alternative data, please keep in mind that this is only one approach to using it, namely, understanding its value in the cross-section of returns. There are many other ways to use alternative data to your advantage, which I cannot even begin to enumerate, lest the scope of this book spiral out of control. However, this approach is probably more useful than the common approach consisting of offering to PMs easy access to "clean" data, without much analytical guidance. You may think that cross-sectional prediction is not enough, and that we should attempt to predict the time-series of returns of a stock based on alternative data. Cross-sectional and time-series prediction are however very closely related, and time-series excess performance can be largely explained by timing the market (see, e.g., [Goyal and Jegadeesh, 2018]). And, as you will see after performing a timing decomposition as in Section 8.2.1, *Timing is Hard.*

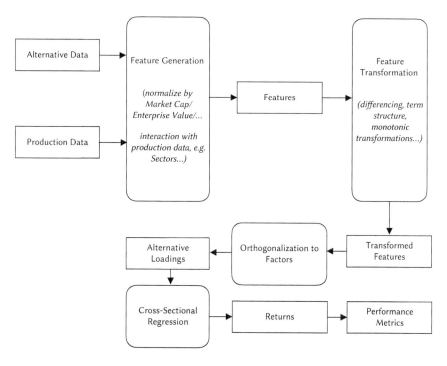

Figure 8.6   Flowchart describing the process connecting alternative data to stock characteristics with potential alpha.

We described the process in broad strokes. A formal description of the process (for quantitative analysts implementing it) is in 11.5. A detailed flowchart of the process is shown in Figure 8.6. Between these two extremes, we provide a familiar example to illustrate the individual steps. The short interest factor is still not included in most commercial risk models. It is of interest to see why. First, prior to March 2007, the SEC required exchange members to provide data only once a month, not twice, making the data more stale. Secondly, Data Explorers became a prominent data source provider of more frequent, globally sourced short interest data around the same time. Hence the data have become available only relatively recently, and academic research on short interest is also more recent than that on other factors. Another reason why short interest is not in most models is that its explanatory power of risk is still debated and that it does not pass tests for factor selection. However, Short Interest is an established alternative data source, since heavily shorted stocks have historically underperformed compared to lightly shorted stocks. Although the size of this anomaly has become smaller after 2017, Short Interest has been available as an alternative data source to informed portfolio managers for well over a decade. In the light of alternative data, let us see how Short Interest is treated as an alternative data source.

1. *Feature Generation:* we covered this in 5.2. Features are borrow rate or short ratio. Sometimes we multiply short interest by a dummy variable representing the sector.
2. *Feature Transformation:* this step is sometimes omitted, in which case we just use the latest value of the short ratio. In the case of short interest, it is sometimes useful to consider the change vs. long-term average, e.g., current short interest against past three-month average.
3. *Orthogonalization:* this can be interpreted as a "cleaning stage": we regress the short interest features against the risk model loadings. Essentially, we try to "explain" short interest using the risk model, and then we keep the component that is *not* explained.
4. *Cross-Sectional Regression:* this step is the same as factor model estimation. The intuition behind this step is to check whether the short-interest loadings and the asset returns are correlated. If they are, then the short-interest return is not zero.
5. *Performance Metrics:* Finally we explore the performance of short interest. Is the expected return non-zero? What is the Sharpe? Do loadings change all the time, so that they are hard to interpret or invest in?

8.5   ★Frequently Asked Questions About Performance

Q: *My performance attribution shows different values from the ones I see in my order management system or performance reports from Treasury. Why?*

A: There may several reasons for this. First, the attribution is computed based on daily returns, based on market close prices and positions. Orders, however, happen intraday. As an extreme case, take the scenario where you open and close a position intraday. Attribution will attribute zero PnL to this stock. This discrepancy is usually categorized as a "trading PnL". Secondly, your PnL is displayed in a specific currency; for simplicity, let us assume dollars. If you are invested in non-US stocks, your PnL in these stocks is the sum of PnL in local currency and of Exchange-Rate Return PnL. If the latter is not perfectly hedged and not displayed as a separate line item, you will see a discrepancy.

Q: *I am long a stock which went up 4% today. Its beta is 1 and the market was up only 1%. So why do I have negative idiosyncratic PnL in this stock?*

A: Because other factors played against the stock. For example, say that the stock is an energy stock, and (a) the energy sector gained 5% in a single day (it has happened); (b) the style factors had negligible returns. Then your stock would have a negative idio PnL, since market and industry factor contributed 6pts to its returns. Sometimes there is more than one factor at play; by summing their contribution you can reconcile total and idiosyncratic PnL.

Q: *When I run any kind of "what-if" analysis and find that my hypothetical strategy has a Sharpe Ratio smaller or greater by x%, how significant are these differences? When I measure Sharpe over a longer period of time, should I give it a higher confidence level?*

A: This is a deep and still-open question. I have two overlapping answers. The first one is that, as Portfolio Manager with a deep expertise in your field, your analysis is confirmatory (or dis-confirmatory). You believe that credit card transactional data give you a better estimate of quarterly revenues; add this information to a stock's score, and then check the result. This is very different from an exploratory analysis, where you try many combinations. Secondly, there are ways to assign a "Sharpe haircut" to a backtested strategy. This is a quantitative topic and you could work with a quantitative analyst to establish some selection principle; standard references are [White, 2000, Hansen and Lunde, 2005, Romano and Wolf, 2005, Harvey and Liu, 2015a,b, Harvey et al., 2016].

8.6   Takeaway Messages

1. Decompose your PnL time series in factor and idiosyncratic.
2. If factor PnL is large, your factor risk is large. You can reduce your future factor risk by optimization, tactical trading (marginally reducing factor risk) or hedging.
3. Decompose your idio time series into timing, sizing and selection skills.
4. If you have positive sizing or timing skill, the Force is with you. Don't fight it.
5. If you don't have sizing, timing of one of them, or both, eliminate their negative impact by equalizing your positions in the appropriate dimension.
6. If your book is large and/or transaction costs are a concern, get help with an automated optimization (as in Appendix 11.6.1).
7. Don't fear optimization. In small doses, it enhances your investment acumen. In large ones, it gives you dependency.
8. Build positions consistently with your alpha horizon and alpha duration. VWAP is a good heuristic. Your current participation rate is probably higher than it should be.
9. Diversify your portfolio as much as you can, but not more than that.
10. Break any of these rules sooner than do anything outright barbarous [Orwell, 1946].

Chapter 9

Manage Your Losses

- *What will you learn here:* Whether you need a stop-loss policy; what are the trade-offs and how do they depend on your performance parameters?
- *Why do you need it:* Because, in the long run, your survival as a fund or portfolio manager *will* depend on setting an effective stop-loss policy. Hence, it is extremely important.
- *When will you need this:* You will set the policy very rarely – usually, only once in the lifetime of a fund. For a portfolio manager, the policy will be binding much less than once a year.

To many readers of this book, loss management is the only form of risk management that matters. "Factors", "alpha", "optimization", "risk limits": these are all modeling constructs; PnL, on the other side, is tangible. A large loss is a threat to the survival of a fund. A simple evasive strategy is to fly from the threat.

149

In an investment strategy, this means liquidating stock holdings into cash. This is often referred to as a "stop-loss" policy. When some threshold is reached, a partial or total liquidation occurs. The rule does not require data or complex models; it is simple; it resonates with human behavior; and it seems *necessary*. Yet, there is no agreement on stop-loss policies. The first section of this chapter is devoted to exploring the arguments in favor and against these policies. The second section connects the design parameters of the policy to the investor's own characteristics and goals. Finally, we look at variants of the rule.

9.1   How Stop-Loss Works

A Portfolio Manager is hired by a hedge fund. The first thing she agrees upon is her budget: how much capital, or how much dollar volatility, she can deploy. The second thing is the loss policy. After the onion of "recommendations" and "portfolio reviews" is peeled, what is left is an estimate of the maximum tolerable loss, after which the PM's portfolio is liquidated. The PM is also usually liquidated, but sometimes is given a second chance. In its simplest form, a stop-loss policy is just this: how much you can lose before it's over. This is hiding many details, however. The starting date from which losses are estimated, for starters. The most common choice is the high water-mark of the strategy; less frequently, losses are measured within a calendar year, and over a 12-month rolling period; throughout the chapter, I focus only on the losses from the high watermark. Besides the single-threshold stop-loss rule, there is a two-threshold variant that is also popular. When the first threshold loss is met, the portfolio is reduced in size; a common choice is 50%. Then if the strategy keeps losing money and reaches a second threshold, the portfolio is finally liquidated. The two-threshold variant is not radically different from the single-threshold one. A prudent portfolio manager would reduce capital as she approaches the liquidation threshold. In an early, important analysis of stop-loss [Grossman and Zhou, 1993] show that, if the PM has the objective to maximize the strategy's expected rate of return while never hitting the loss threshold, then it is optimal to hold a GMV that is at its upper bound on a high watermark, but it is proportionally reduced as the distance to the stop-loss threshold is reduced, and is fully liquidated to cash when the threshold is reached.[1] The rationale for the more complex variant is that it enforces this discipline.

Stop-loss procedures can be further classified into two types:

- **Stop-and-Shutdown**. When a portfolio reaches the final loss threshold, it is definitely liquidated and the strategy is shut down permanently.
- **Stop-and-Restart**. When a portfolio reaches the final loss threshold, it is liquidated but the positions are still updated and the pro forma performance of the strategy is still monitored. When it recovers (i.e., has a return exceeding a certain hurdle), the portfolio is capitalized again and starts trading.

As always, there is not a hard separation between these two procedures. Within the same firm, a PM with a long track record is stopped and then restarted, while a new one is not given the benefit of the doubt.

9.2   Why a Stop-Loss Policy?

We review the rationales behind this rule and its drawbacks.

These are the arguments in favor.

- **There is the stop-loss that you have, and the one you don't know you have**. The difference between a firm with a stop-loss policy and one without is that you find out about the stop-loss policy of the latter when it is too late. But rest assured that they *always* do have one. It may be discretionary; it may be PM-specific; it may be truly inscrutable and non-replicable, but it exists. What is at issue then is whether it should be transparent or not. My experience is that almost all PMs would be in favor of transparency, and almost all hedge fund managers would be against, even though they insist that they don't really have one and *this is good for you*. As a rule

---

[1] Two secondary observations: 1. the optimal GMV rule is not exactly proportional, but it is very well approximated by it; 2. since this is an idealized model, the threshold is actually never reached and capital is never set exactly to zero.

of wisdom, don't trust any hedge fund manager who tells you that something is good for you unless that hedge fund manager is your mother.[2] And because stop-loss rules exist, you may as well understand whether its parameters suit your investment profile or not, which is the subject of the remainder of the chapter.

- **Stop-loss rules are a partial hedge for the PM call option.** If a PM is paid for performance in full every year, without deferred compensation and any clawbacks,[3] then she holds a call option on the underlying value of her strategy. The strike price is higher than the initial value of the portfolio, because the PM must recover operating costs; the payoff is not the PnL of the portfolio but a percentage of it, with some kickers for high performance or high risk-adjusted performance. Since the value of the option increases with the volatility of the underlying asset, it is in the interest of the manager to run with the highest possible volatility, independently of her skill. The stop-loss is a constraint that limits the value of this option. If the PM has poor investing skill, her portfolio's PnL will get closer to a threshold. In order to still be able to trade she will reduce her volatility, a phenomenon that is intuitive, confirmed in practice and justified by some theory that we will discuss below. By reducing volatility, the value of the call option is reduced.
- **Stop-losses can be interpreted as a form of portfolio insurance.** Consider the case in which the PM buys full downside insurance in the form of an out-of-the-money put option on the portfolio value, with notional value equal to the maximum GMV limit. It can be shown that the option can be approximately replicated by a combination of the portfolio and cash that is close to the drawdown policy. There are differences between the "ideal" policy, the proportional policy, the put policy and the two-threshold policy,[4] and they are shown in Figure 9.1. The Grossman-Zhou proportional policy is the most aggressive: it starts reducing immediately. The

---

[2] Correction: except when your mother asks you to sign a contract. Then don't trust her.

[3] "Clawbacks" are conditions according to which a PM's deferred compensation is reduced if she loses money in a year.

[4] Let the portfolio have high watermark value S_0. Having a stop-loss at loss r is equivalent to holding the portfolio and purchasing a put with strike price $K = S_0(1 - r)$. At time t the portfolio has value S and the option has value $V(S)$; the put is equivalent

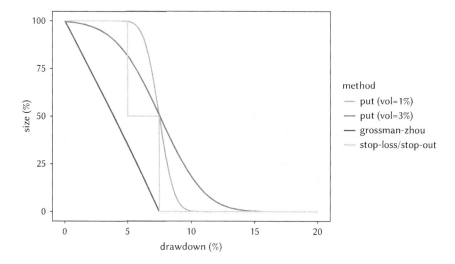

Figure 9.1 Deployed Capital as a function of drawdown for Grossman-Zhou optimal growth rule, portfolio insurance for two strategies with daily volatilities of 1% and 3%, and for a two-threshold policy, as adopted in many hedge funds.

portfolio insurance policy depends on the volatility of the underlying strategy. A more volatile strategy must reduce earlier, but can hold capital beyond the stop-loss, because greater volatility means that the strategy has greater optionality. A less volatile strategy is "stiffer": it reduces later but faster.[5] Finally, the two-threshold policy can be "tuned" to approximate any stop-loss curve.

In summary: provided that a strict limit to losses always exists, a GMV reduction policy that decreases as the distance from the max

---

to a cash position and amount

$$\delta(S) = \frac{\partial V}{\partial S}(S)$$

Hence the effective portfolio size is $S + \delta(S)$. The policy for Grossman and Zhou is $f = S_0(1 - r/(S_0 - S))$.

[5] Sometimes you'll hear the expression that stop-loss policies have "negative gamma". This is a way of saying that the value of the embedded put option, as a function of the underlying, is a convex function: its second derivative with respect to the underlying is negative. This is actually true in the first part of portfolio reduction only, but the initial portfolio reduction is what occurs most often and therefore matters most.

loss decreases is both intuitive and justified by some quantitative models. What are the arguments against a stop-loss policy?

- **Transaction costs can be significant**. Executing the strategy requires reducing the Gross Market Value of the book independently from fundamental considerations (like an increase or reduction in investment opportunities). As an example, a PM has a turnover of 12/year, measured as the ratio of dollars traded in a year/GMV. He incurs losses and reduces GMV by 50% and grows it back 1 month later. The turnover is 11x (the eleven months during a normal regime) + 0.5x (the one month run at 50% GMV) + 1x (the de- and re-grossing). This is an increase of 5%, and a larger increase expressed as transaction costs, because the individual trades in a partial liquidation are much larger than routine trades. Stop-losses don't occur every year; however, the implementation cost of the policy, averaged over the years, is non-negligible and must be assessed (e.g., by simulation).

- **The opportunity costs can be large**. This is the most important objection to stop-losses. By cutting capital in a drawdown, we are less well-positioned to exploit the recovery phase. We are forgoing PnL. There are papers (mostly theoretical, and with little empirical basis) that show how, if certain assumptions hold, then stop-loss policies will make money for the PM. For example, if past positive PnL is a predictor of future positive PnL (and vice-versa), then you can imagine how the policy helps: if I am losing money and therefore will lose money, it is better to reduce now to avoid incurring future losses. However, these papers miss the point. Stop-loss exists to ensure survival of a firm, not to improve the performance of a strategy. There is a price to pay. We just need to make sure we are not overpaying, or at least that we understand the trade-off between survivability and the parameters of stop-loss.

9.3   The Costs and Benefits of Stop-Loss

A shallow stop-loss threshold reduces profitability; a large one is ineffective at managing risk. Is there a "Goldilocks" region in which stop-loss reduces risk without affecting performance? To explore this question, I resort to simulation. Consider PMs with a fixed annualized volatility and an annualized dollar volatility. I simulate PMs' returns with a range of Sharpe Ratios and a range of stop losses. For each PM and for every simulation I measure two important metrics:

- The ratio of the average annual PnL over the entire horizon to the strategy's dollar volatility *when the strategy is active*. I denote this ratio "efficiency". This is not the same as the realized Sharpe Ratio. If a PM is stopped at the end of year one, and we simulate a period of ten years, the realized volatility of years two to ten is zero, and the PnL is zero. This is misrepresenting the performance of the strategy, so we measure the average PnL of the entire ten years over the *allocated* volatility during the same interval;
- The ratio of stop-loss limit to allocated vol. This measure is natural. We often speak of a "two sigma" loss to mean that the dollar loss was equal to twice the dollar volatility allocated to a strategy.

To make the simulation more comprehensive, I consider two operating horizons: five and ten years; not many PMs operate in the same firm for ten years, but it is important to understand how the horizon affects the results. I consider two stop-loss policies: a single-threshold one (liquidate the strategy at $x\%$ loss) and a two-threshold one (cut capital in half when loss reaches $(x/2)\%$, and liquidate at $x\%$ loss). To approximate heavy-tailed returns, which can matter in this context, returns distribution in the simulation is not Gaussian, but a Student with 6 degrees of freedom. The results are shown in Figure 9.2. There is a great deal of useful information in these charts.

- For a fixed value of the ratio max % loss to % annualized vol, the PnL to allocated vol is *always* smaller than the Sharpe Ratio, which is shown as a horizontal dotted line. This is intuitive. To control maximum loss there is a loss in risk-adjusted performance.
- The PnL to allocated vol is *always* smaller in the ten-year simulation than in the five-year one. This is also intuitive. When we stop a PM with, say a Sharpe Ratio equal to one, we forgo a larger PnL in the ten-year case.
- The price of safety is higher for lower-Sharpe PMs than higher-Sharpe ones. You can see this in the steeper slope of the curve for high-Sharpe PMs. And this is intuitive. A two-Sharpe PM is not stopped as often as a one-Sharpe PM.

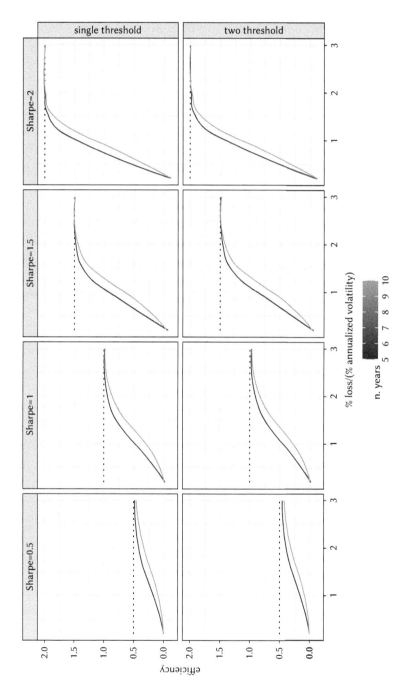

Figure 9.2 Impact of stop-loss on performance. We visualize five- and ten-year investment horizons.

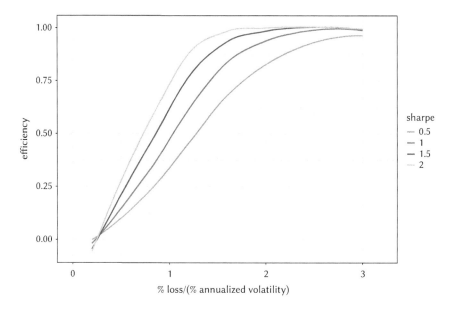

Figure 9.3   Relationship between efficiency of a strategy and stop-loss, based on five-year simulations.

- The difference between single-threshold and two-threshold stop-loss policies is negligible, a confirmation that the main benefit of the two-threshold policy is to encourage discipline in the liquidation process.

While Figure 9.2 is useful to understand the qualitative relationship between the many parameters that, in addition to stop-loss, affect realized performance, it is hard to derive some quantitative recommendations from them. Figure 9.3 addresses this issue. I focus on a five-year interval and on a single-threshold rule; this is closer to the typical tenure of a PM in a firm; in addition, the Sharpe Ratio of a PM should be reevaluated on a horizon of three to five years. The graph shows on the y axis, the ratio between the "realized performance" used in Figure 9.2, and the true Sharpe Ratio of the PM. We call this ratio the *efficiency* of the stop-loss rule. On the x axis is the stop-loss threshold, as a fraction of the PM's volatility. As a general rule, the stricter the stop-loss rule, the greater the loss in efficiency; however, the efficiency loss is (a) nonlinear in the normalized stop-loss threshold; (b) depends heavily on the Sharpe Ratio of the PM. Table 9.1

Table 9.1 Efficiency for different values of the PM Sharpe Ratio and the loss/vol ratio.

	Loss/Vol					
Sharpe	1	1.2	1.4	1.6	1.8	2
0.50	0.33	0.47	0.58	0.69	0.76	0.83
1.00	0.47	0.62	0.75	0.85	0.90	0.93
1.50	0.64	0.79	0.88	0.93	0.97	0.98
2.00	0.78	0.88	0.96	0.98	0.99	1.00

presents some of the efficiency data. If we set a normalized stop-loss threshold of 1.4, the efficiency is 96% for a PM with a Sharpe Ratio of 2, but only 58% for a PM with a Sharpe Ratio of 0.5. In other terms, we can interpret the curves in Figure 9.3 thus: the trade-off is initially steeper for high-Sharpe PMs, as shown by the fact that the purple line has a larger slope than the red one, but the trade-off is less likely to affect the PM, because for typical values of the stop-loss thresholds (say, between 150% and 250% of the PM's volatility) a high-Sharpe PM is unlikely to be affected while a low-Sharpe PM will suffer a sizable efficiency loss. What lesson can we draw from this? The price of certain downside protection is high. A PM with a native Sharpe Ratio of 1 and a stop loss equal to 1.5 times her volatility has a realized Sharpe of 0.8. If the firm has four PMs with this performance and uncorrelated returns, the realized Sharpe (before fees) goes from 2 to 1.6.

9.4 Takeaway Messages

1. Explicit or implicit, stop-loss rules are ubiquitous and necessary.
2. They serve several purposes:
   - As a form of put option to offset the call option owned by the PM.
   - As a form of tail portfolio insurance.

3. Stop-loss rules have two drawbacks:
   - Transaction costs due to trading induced by de-grossing and re-grossing portfolios.
   - Performance degradation due to forgone profits.
4. Differences between the simple rule of single-threshold and two-threshold stop-loss are small.
5. Performance degradation is a bigger concern than transaction costs. Choose the stop-loss threshold for your strategy or for PMs in your firm, based on trade-off curves in the chapters.

Chapter 10

★Set Your Leverage Ratio for a Sustainable Business

- *What will you learn here:* What leverage to set for your fund.
- *Why do you need it:* If you are starting a fund, this is perhaps the most important decision you take. It will determine whether the fund can meet its return and risk goals.
- *When will you need this:* You will need this chapter only when you decide to start a fund, and when your fund undergoes structural changes, like an increase in the number of PMs, geographical coverage, breadth, or investment style.

Leverage Decisions are usually not under the control of a portfolio manager, the exception being when the portfolio manager is also the principal of the firm. Therefore, it is unlikely that this section will be relevant to you, the exception being that it may be the *most* relevant section to you in the entire book, in which case I recommend plodding through the math. Although I am going to analyze this problem only from a risk perspective, I would like to point out that there are additional dimensions to it. On the one side, the Treasury department would look at funding adequacy and set an upper limit to leverage based on its counterparty agreements, a detailed simulation of margin rules and worst-case scenarios. On the other side, the strategic positioning of a firm compared to its peers is essential to its success. The value proposition of the firm determines the parameters that determine leverage in the present and set the direction for its future risk posture. Even through the narrow path of risk, this is a complex answer. How should leverage ratio be defined? What are the drivers of the leverage ratio? We make a few assumptions.

1. The portfolio has negligible factor variance;
2. The stocks have all the same percentage idio volatility, which we denote with the symbol σ;
3. The portfolio has Sharpe Ratio s;
4. All n individual stocks positions have the same invested capital;
5. The borrow cost is zero.

It is relatively straightforward to extend the model. Stocks don't have the same idio volatility: we can get around that through more refined approximations or numerical simulations. Cost of borrowing is not zero, but we can adjust the formulas for it, too. The rationale behind this choice of assumptions is that it is the minimum viable model for thinking about leverage. If you find the derivation of the final result too unwieldy, you can go straight to Formula 10.5 and then slowly work your way back. Mathematics, like life, must be applied forward, but can be understood backward.

10.1   A Framework for Leverage Decisions

Define *leverage* as the ratio L of Gross Market Value to Assets Under Management (AUM):

$$L = \frac{GMV}{AUM}$$

Other definitions differ from this one by a constant (e.g., ratio of Long Market Value to AUM).

The *ratio of portfolio dollar volatility to GMV* is given by[1]

$$\frac{(single\ stock\ percentage\ idio\ vol)}{\sqrt{(number\ of\ stocks)}} = \frac{\sigma}{\sqrt{n}}$$

For example, a portfolio with 70 stocks and single stock idio vol of 20% has a \$vol/GMV=2.4%: a portfolio with GMV=\$1B has \$30M of volatility.

The expected PnL of a portfolio is given by

$$s \times (portfolio\ dollar\ volatility)$$

where s is the Sharpe Ratio; hence

$$(expected\ PnL) = s \times \frac{\sigma}{\sqrt{n}} \times GMV$$

The return is the expected PnL divided by AUM:

$$(return) = s \times \frac{\sigma}{\sqrt{n}} \times GMV \times \frac{L}{GMV}$$

$$= s \times \frac{\sigma}{\sqrt{n}} \times L \tag{10.1}$$

Therefore, if we want to achieve a minimum return before fees, we have to satisfy the inequality *(expected return)* ≥ *(min return)*, and this implies that

$$L \geq \frac{\sqrt{n}}{\sigma} \times \frac{(min\ return)}{s} \tag{10.2}$$

---

[1] Proof in the Appendix.

For example, say that $n = 100$, $\sigma = 20\%$ and $s = 1.5$. We target an annualized return of 15%, then $L \geq 5$. Another example: $n = 500$, $\sigma = 20\%$ and $s = 2.5$. We still target 15% annualized return. Then $L \geq 6.7$. A fund with large breadth, say $n = 500$, and mediocre Sharpe Ratio (for a long-short hedge fund), say $s = 1.5$, will be forced to have a high leverage: with these numbers, L must exceed 11.2. The important messages of Formula (10.2) are that:

• It gives a lower bound on leverage;
• The parameters n, σ and s cannot be changed – they are features of the strategy;
• The minimum leverage is proportional to minimum return;
• Everything being equal, the higher the Sharpe, the lower the leverage.

The problem of high leverage is the increased risk of a high drawdown. Consider the annualized return of the strategy. It is approximately distributed as a normal random variable, with expected value given by Equation (10.1), i.e., $s \times (\sigma/\sqrt{n}) \times L$, and with volatility equal to $(\sigma/\sqrt{n}) \times L$. However, in large drawdown events, it is always the case that the realized volatility is a multiple of the predicted volatility; investors experience two, three, even six sigma events. Residual portfolio volatility doesn't present the same realized shock levels as factor volatility: as we discussed in Section 7.2, factors are shocked far more than idio. In any case, this is an instance in which we need to deviate from theory and assume that realized portfolio volatility is inflated by a positive factor κ: $(portfolio\ volatility) = \kappa \times \sigma \times L/\sqrt{n}$, where κ is a constant, which we set based on experience, with values between 1 (if we really believe in models) and 3 (if we are skeptical).

How much of an annualized loss are we willing to tolerate, and with which probability? This depends on the risk appetite of the fund's investors, and on the track record of the fund itself. Losing 5% of AUM in the first year of life of a fund is more compromising than losing 20% after a ten-year successful track record. And what should the max probability p_{loss} of this loss be? A reasonable value for p_{loss} is 1%, even better 0.1%. Intuitively, the higher the leverage, the riskier the fund; therefore our requirements on maximum loss and probability force an upper limit on leverage.

The formula that bounds the leverage from above is[2]

$$L \le \frac{\sqrt{n}}{\sigma} \times \frac{(\textit{max d.d.\%})}{-\kappa F^{-1}(p_{\text{loss}}) - s} \qquad (10.3)$$

where $F^{-1}(p)$ is the quantile function of the standard normal distribution and is negative for probability values lower than 50%: $F^{-1}(0.05) = -1.6$, $F^{-1}(0.01) = -2.3$, and $F^{-1}(0.001) = -3.1$. In practice, we want to set $-\kappa F^{-1}(p_{\text{loss}})$ between 4 and 6.

This formula also is intuitive:

- The maximum leverage is proportional to maximum drawdown, as it should be;
- Everything being equal, to a higher Sharpe Ratio corresponds a higher maximum leverage;
- If the Sharpe Ratio exceeds $-\kappa F^{-1}(p_{\text{loss}})$, then the admissible leverage has no upper bound.

Now we have a floor and a ceiling on leverage:

$$\frac{\sqrt{n}}{\sigma} \times \frac{(\textit{min return})}{s} \le L \le \frac{\sqrt{n}}{\sigma} \times \frac{(\textit{max d.d.\%})}{-\kappa F^{-1}(p_{\text{loss}}) - s} \qquad (10.4)$$

We can make this concrete by assuming probability of drawdown equal to 2.5% and a shock constant $\kappa = 2$. We can replace the rather cryptic $\kappa F^{-1}(p_{\text{dd}})$ with -4:

$$\frac{\sqrt{n}}{\sigma} \times \frac{(\textit{min return})}{s} \le L \le \frac{\sqrt{n}}{\sigma} \times \frac{(\textit{max d.d.})}{4 - s}$$

---

[2] The requirement on the drawdown occurring with probability less than p_{loss} is

$$P\left(\frac{s\sigma L}{\sqrt{n}} + \frac{\kappa \sigma L}{\sqrt{n}}\xi \le -(\textit{max d.d.\%})\right) = P\left(\xi \le -\frac{s}{\kappa} - \frac{\sqrt{n}}{\kappa \sigma L}(\textit{max d.d.\%})\right)$$

$$= F\left(-\frac{s}{\kappa} - \frac{\sqrt{n}}{\kappa \sigma L}(\textit{max d.d.\%})\right)$$

$$\le p_{\text{loss}}$$

where ξ is a standard Gaussian random variable. Isolate L to obtain Formula (10.3). Note that if $s > -\kappa F^{-1}(p_{\text{loss}})$, then the inequality is satisfied for any value of L.

Table 10.1   Ranges for Leverage Ratio. Values of max leverage are highlighted in **bold** when there is no feasible range for the leverage that meets both requirements.

n.stocks	Sharpe	min return	max d.d.	min lev.	max lev.
100	1	15	10	7.50	**1.67**
100	1.5	15	10	5.00	**2.00**
100	2	15	10	3.75	**2.50**
100	2.5	15	10	3.00	3.33
100	1	15	15	7.50	**2.50**
100	1.5	15	15	5.00	**3.00**
100	2	15	15	3.75	3.75
100	2.5	15	15	3.00	3.50
200	1	15	10	10.6	**2.36**
200	1.5	15	10	7.07	**2.82**
200	2	15	10	5.30	**3.53**
200	2.5	15	10	4.24	4.71
200	1	15	15	10.6	**3.53**
200	1.5	15	15	7.07	**4.24**
200	2	15	15	5.30	5.30
200	2.5	15	15	4.24	7.07

In Table 10.1 you can see some numerical examples. Aside from the values themselves, there is another message in Equation (10.4): it is possible that the lower bound on leverage is bigger than the upper bound. You can interpret this scenario as one in which the hedge fund is not sustainable from a risk perspective. Given the parameters of the fund (Sharpe, breadth, volatility of the coverage universe) and the performance and risk requirements (annualized returns and max annualized drawdown), there is no leverage that meets these requirements. You could read this scenario as a potential explanation of "why so many hedge funds fail". From a different angle, you could read the equation for an explanation of the sustainability of multi-manager platforms. Their Sharpe Ratio before fees is very high (in fact, close to or greater than 4), which enables them to be highly leveraged. Finally, the formula is also compatible with the business model of the "tiger cubs". These funds have very low breadth (an effective number of assets sometimes smaller than 10), invest in high-volatility stocks, have a Sharpe between 0.5 and 1, and have high tolerance for drawdowns. With these parameters, the lower and upper bounds on leverage are $(1, 1.5)$.

One last important point: if we combine the main formula in this answer with the relationship between Sharpe Ratio and Information Ratio we covered in Section 7.2.1, we can understand why it is so important to have a higher percentage idio p_{idio}: because it improves the SR of a portfolio, allowing sufficient leverage. Let us use the IR instead of the Sharpe:

$$\frac{\sqrt{n}}{\sigma} \times \frac{(min\ return)}{\sqrt{p_{\text{idio}}} \times (Inf.\ Ratio)} \leq L \leq \frac{\sqrt{n}}{\sigma} \times \frac{(max\ d\ .d.\ \%)}{4 - \sqrt{p_{\text{idio}}} \times (Inf.\ Ratio)}$$
$$(10.5)$$

When the percentage idio p_{idio} increases, it works its magic on both sides of the equation: the lower admissible leverage decreases and the highest admissible leverage increases. The fact that the interval is wider gives an additional margin of safety: even if some of the parameters in the formula are inaccurate, it is more likely that you will meet the requirements on returns and drawdown.

10.2   Takeaway Messages

1. The sustainable leverage ratio is primarily a function of five parameters:
   (a) Target returns;
   (b) Maximum acceptable loss;
   (c) Portfolio breadth;
   (d) Asset volatility;
   (e) Sharpe Ratio.
   You can choose the first two; the last three are characteristics of your investment style and asset coverage.
2. Target returns determine leverage's lower bound; leverage is a return multiplier.

3. Maximum acceptable loss determines leverage's upper bound.
4. Breadth, volatility and Sharpe Ratio tie the two together.
5. To achieve long-term sustainability, make sure that at any time leverage is compatible with your fund's parameters; Formula (10.4) provides bounds.

Chapter 11

★★Appendix

11.1 Essential Risk Model Formulas

Here we collect the most important equations and identities.

11.1.1 *Factor Model*

We have n assets, m factors. Time is discrete. The master equation of returns according to factor models is

$$\mathbf{r}_t = \alpha + \mathbf{B}_t \mathbf{f}_t + \epsilon_t$$

where

$\mathbf{r}_t$: n-dimensional vector of asset total returns;
α : n-dimensional vector of expected returns;
ϵ_t : n-dimensional vector of asset idio returns;
$\mathbf{f}_t$: m-dimensional vector of factor returns;
$\mathbf{B}_t$: $n \times m$ matrix of factor loadings.

In all models, m is much smaller than n. The vectors $\mathbf{f}_t$ and ϵ_t and multivariate normal random variables with covariance matrices $\boldsymbol{\Omega}_{f,t} \in R^{m \times m}$ and $\boldsymbol{\Omega}_{\epsilon,t} \in R^{n \times n}$: $\mathbf{f}_t \sim N(0, \boldsymbol{\Omega}_{f,t})$, $\epsilon_t \sim N(0, \boldsymbol{\Omega}_{\epsilon,t})$; in applications $\boldsymbol{\Omega}_\epsilon$ is sparse and often diagonal. It follows that the asset covariance matrix is the sum of a low-rank matrix and a sparse one:

$$\boldsymbol{\Omega}_{r,t} = \mathbf{B}_t \boldsymbol{\Omega}_{f,t} \mathbf{B}_t' + \boldsymbol{\Omega}_{\epsilon,t}$$

11.1.2 Factor-Mimicking Portfolios

In the case of fundamental model, we are given the loadings matrix B and estimate the factor returns. The estimation problem is a weighted least-squares:

$$\min \ (\mathbf{r} - \mathbf{Bf})'\mathbf{W}(\mathbf{r} - \mathbf{Bf})$$

$$\text{s.t. } \mathbf{f} \in \mathbb{R}^m$$

The matrix $\mathbf{W}$ is diagonal and positive definite. If we knew the idiosyncratic covariance matrix $\boldsymbol{\Omega}_\epsilon$ in advance, then setting $\mathbf{W} = \boldsymbol{\Omega}_\epsilon^{-1}$ results in an unbiased estimator $\mathbf{f}$ with the lowest estimation error. Since we do not know this matrix in advance, in practical applications a proxy for the inverse of the idiosyncratic variances are the weights $W_{ii} = (\text{market cap}_i)^{1/2}$, where the market cap of the stock is averaged over a number of days (say, 21 trading days). The solution is given by

$$\hat{\mathbf{f}} = (\mathbf{B}'\mathbf{WB})^{-1}\mathbf{BWr}$$

$$\hat{\epsilon} = (I - \mathbf{B}(\mathbf{B}'\mathbf{WB})^{-1}\mathbf{B}'\mathbf{W})\mathbf{r}$$

The estimated vector return $\hat{f}_i$ is equal to the scalar product of the ith row of the matrix

$$\mathbf{V}' = (\mathbf{B}'\mathbf{WB})^{-1}\mathbf{B}'\mathbf{W}$$

and the return vector. We can interpret the matrix row as a vector of portfolio weights; this portfolio has return $\hat{f}_i$. It is called the *factor-mimicking portfolio* $\mathbf{v}_i$ for factor i; we denote $\mathbf{V}$ the matrix whose ith column is $\mathbf{v}_i$. It can be shown that this portfolio is the solution of an optimization problem: find the minimum-variance portfolio that has unit exposure to factor i and zero exposure to any other factor. This portfolio is the best tracking portfolio of the factor, because its returns are $\mathbf{v}_i'\mathbf{r} = f_i + $ (*noise with the smallest possible volatility*). The noise term should not be ignored. To estimate it, we make the assumption that $\mathbf{W} = \Omega_e^{-1}$. Then

$$\hat{\mathbf{f}} = (\mathbf{B}'\Omega_e^{-1}\mathbf{B})^{-1}\mathbf{B}'\Omega_e^{-1}\mathbf{r}$$
$$= (\mathbf{B}'\Omega_e^{-1}\mathbf{B})^{-1}\mathbf{B}'\Omega_e^{-1}(\mathbf{Bf} + \epsilon)$$
$$= \mathbf{f} + (\mathbf{B}'\Omega_e^{-1}\mathbf{B})^{-1}\mathbf{B}'\Omega_e^{-1}\epsilon$$
$$\Rightarrow \Omega_{\hat{\mathbf{f}}} = \Omega_{\mathbf{f}} + (\mathbf{B}'\Omega_e^{-1}\mathbf{B})^{-1} \qquad\qquad (11.1)$$

11.1.3 Percentage Idio Variance

Given a portfolio $\mathbf{w} \in \mathbb{R}^n$, define the factor exposures $\mathbf{b} = \mathbf{B}'\mathbf{w}$.

$$\mathbf{w}'\Omega_r\mathbf{w} = \mathbf{b}'\Omega_f\mathbf{b} \qquad + \qquad \mathbf{w}'\Omega_e\mathbf{w}$$
$$(\textit{factor var}) \qquad + \qquad (\textit{idio var})$$

The percentage idio variance is

$$\frac{\mathbf{w}'\Omega_e\mathbf{w}}{\mathbf{b}'\Omega_f\mathbf{b} + \mathbf{w}'\Omega_e\mathbf{w}}$$

11.1.4 Betas

Consider a benchmark with weights $\mathbf{v} \in \mathbb{R}^n$ for its components. The weights are positive and sum to one. The predicted beta of a portfolio $\mathbf{v} \in \mathbb{R}^n$ to the benchmark is

$$\beta(\mathbf{w}, \mathbf{v}) = \frac{\mathbf{w}'\Omega_r\mathbf{v}}{\mathbf{v}'\Omega_r\mathbf{v}}$$

11.1.5 Marginal Contribution to Factor Risk

The marginal contribution to factor risk is defined as the derivative of factor risk with respect to asset i. It is equal to

$$\mathrm{MCFR}_i = \frac{\partial}{\partial w_i}\sqrt{\mathbf{w}'\mathbf{B}\Omega_f\mathbf{B}'\mathbf{w}}$$
$$= \frac{[\mathbf{B}\Omega_f\mathbf{b}]_i}{\sqrt{\mathbf{b}'\Omega_f\mathbf{b}}}$$

11.2 Diversification

To illustrate the relationship between Information Ratio, diversification and hitting rate, we consider the following setting:

- We have two periods. Investment occurs in the first period and returns are realized in the second one.
- We invest in N stocks. The NMV invested in stock i is w_i.
- We assume, for the sake of simplicity, that stocks have normally distributed residual returns r_i with identical volatility σ.
- There is a "hitting probability" p, which is the probability of guessing correctly the sign of the daily return of a stock: $p = P(r_i w_i > 0)$.

The expected idiosyncratic PnL of the portfolio is

$$E\left(\sum_{i=1}^{N} r_i w_i\right) = \sum_{i=1}^{N} |w_i| \times E|r_i| \times P(\mathrm{sgn}(w_i r_i > 0) - \mathrm{sgn}(w_i r_i < 0))$$

$$= E|r_i|(2p-1)\sum_i E|w_i|$$

$$= \sigma\sqrt{\frac{2}{\pi}}(2p-1)\sum_i |w_i|$$

The expected volatility of the portfolio is

$$\left(\sum_{i=1}^{N} w_i^2 \sigma^2\right)^{1/2} = \sigma\left(\sum_{i=1}^{N} w_i^2\right)^{1/2}$$

$$IR = (2p-1)\sqrt{\frac{2}{\pi}}\frac{\sum_i |w_i|}{\left(\sum_{i=1}^{N} w_i^2\right)^{1/2}} = (2p-1)\sqrt{\frac{2}{\pi}}\sqrt{N_{\mathrm{eff}}}$$

And the annualized IR is $(2p-1)\sqrt{N_{\mathrm{eff}}}\sqrt{2 \times 252/\pi} \simeq 12.6 \times (2p-1)$ $\sqrt{N_{\mathrm{eff}}}$. The quantity N_{eff} is the *effective number of stocks*[1]:

$$N_{\mathrm{eff}} = \frac{(\sum_i |w_i|)^2}{\sum_{i=1}^{N} w_i^2} = \frac{||\mathbf{w}||_1^2}{||\mathbf{w}||_2^2} \tag{11.2}$$

---

[1] Below we denote norm $||\mathbf{x}||_a = (\sum_i |x_i|^a)^{1/a}$.

To get some intuition we express the portfolio positions as weights relative to the GMV of the portfolio: $\hat{w}_i = w_i/GMV$. All x_i are between 0 and 1, and sum to 1. A well-known measure of concentration of the vector x_i is the Herfindahl index $H = \sum_i \hat{x}_i^2$. When the portfolio consists of only one stock the index is equal to 1; when the portfolio has identically sized positions the index is equal to $1/N$. The effective number of stocks is equal to the inverse of the Herfindahl index:

$$N_e = \frac{1}{H(\mathbf{w})}$$

and therefore ranges between 1 and N.

The formula generalizes to the case where stocks have no identical idio volatilities. In that case we replace w_i with $\sigma_i w_i$, the dollar idio vol allocated to stock i.

11.3   Mean-Variance Formulations

The objective of this section is to summarize basic results in mean-variance optimization, and to assess the impact of uncertainty of alphas on the solutions. We use these results in simple asset allocation problems (e.g., determine the size of market exposure in an ideal portfolio), and for alpha sizing analysis.

11.3.1   Mean-Variance Portfolios

Consider the usual factor model, with excess returns α and covariance matrix $\mathbf{\Omega}_r = \mathbf{B}\mathbf{\Omega}_f\mathbf{B}' + \mathbf{\Omega}_e$. The mean-variance problem is:

$$\max \; \alpha' x - \frac{1}{2\rho} x' \mathbf{\Omega}_r x$$

which is solved by $x = \rho\mathbf{\Omega}_r^{-1}\alpha$

There is a more intuitive interpretation of the solution. Let $\mathbf{V}$ be a diagonal matrix containing the asset volatilies, and let $\mathbf{C}$ be the asset correlation matrix. Then the asset covariance matrix is $\mathbf{\Omega}_r = \mathbf{V}\mathbf{C}\mathbf{V}$ and $\mathbf{\Omega}_r^{-1} = \mathbf{V}^{-1}\mathbf{C}^{-1}\mathbf{V}^{-1}$, so we can rewrite the solution as

$$\mathbf{V}x = \rho\mathbf{C}^{-1}(\mathbf{V}^{-1}\alpha)$$

Vx is the vector of the optimal dollar volatilities **v** allocated to the assets. $V^{-1}\alpha$ is the vector of the Sharpe Ratios **s** of the individual assets. Therefore

$$\mathbf{v} = \rho\mathbf{C}^{-1}\mathbf{s}$$

If the assets are uncorrelated, then the optimal dollar volatility allocation is proportional to the Sharpe Ratios of the assets.

The simplest application of this formula is in the case of two uncorrelated assets. For example, the first asset is the portfolio held by a portfolio manager and the second is a market index. Ratio of the optimal dollar volatility of the market index to the dollar portfolio volatility is

$$\frac{market\ var}{total\ var} = \frac{s_m^2}{s_m^2 + s_p^2} = \frac{1}{1 + (s_p/s_m)^2}$$

This is the formula we show in Section 7.2.2. We extend this formula to Gross Market Values. If σ_m, σ_p are the percentage volatilities for market and portfolio respectively, then

$$\frac{g_m}{g_p} = \frac{\sigma_p s_m}{\sigma_m s_p} \text{ from which } \frac{g_m}{g_p + g_m} = \frac{1}{1 + \frac{\sigma_m s_p}{\sigma_p s_m}}$$

11.3.2   A Robust Mean-Variance Formulation

As we mentioned in Chapter 6, in practice Mean-Variance Optimization does not produce the performance we would expect. To remedy MVO's shortcomings, Robust Portfolio Optimization relaxes the assumptions of the basic theory. Developed over the past 20 years, this is still an active area of research. I refer the reader to the monograph [Fabozzi et al., 2007] and the surveys [Kolm et al., 2014, Xidonas et al., 2020]. Here we follow the simple approach of [Stubbs and Vance, 2005] to justify the empirical observation that using a shrinked covariance matrix outperforms the naïve approach. Let $\alpha \sim N(\mu_\alpha, \Omega_\alpha)$. The mean-variance optimization problem now has an additional term generated by alpha's randomness:

$$\max E[(\alpha + \mathbf{B}f\epsilon)'\mathbf{x}] - \frac{1}{2\rho}\text{stdev}[(\alpha + \mathbf{B}f + \epsilon)'\mathbf{x}]$$

This is equal to

$$\max \; \mu_\alpha' \mathbf{x} - \frac{1}{2\rho}\mathbf{x}'(\Omega_\alpha + \Omega_r)\mathbf{x}$$

Hence the solution is given by

$$\mathbf{x} = \rho(\Omega_\alpha + \Omega_r)^{-1}\mu_\alpha$$

And the optimum is

$$\frac{\rho}{2}\mu_\alpha'(\Omega_\alpha + \Omega_r)^{-1}\mu_\alpha$$

If $\Omega_\alpha = \tau^2 I$, then the solution is given by $\mathbf{x} = \rho(\Omega_r + \tau^2 I)^{-1}\mu_\alpha$. If we add the constraint $\mathbf{B}'\mathbf{x} = 0$ (no factor risk), the solution simplifies to

$$x_i = \frac{[\mu_\alpha]_i}{[\sigma_\epsilon]_i^2 + \tau^2}$$

For $\tau = 0$, this gives the MVO sizing rule; for $\tau \to \infty$ this gives the equal-sized rule.

It is possible to obtain the same solution starting from different assumptions. The first one is the linear Ledoit-Wolf shrinked covariance matrix approach [Ledoit and Wolf, 2003]. The second one is the assumption that the excess returns are uncertain but bound to lie within an ellipsoid centered at μ_α. The optimization problem aims to maximize the worst-case mean-variance:

$$\max_{\mathbf{x}} \; \min_\alpha \alpha'\mathbf{x} - \frac{1}{2\rho}\mathbf{x}'\Omega_r\mathbf{x}$$

$$\text{s.t. } (\alpha - \mu_\alpha)'(\alpha - \mu_\alpha) \le L$$

11.4   Proportional-Rule Formulations

Let α be the vector of expected returns and let g be a target GMV. We want to find the holdings that are closest (in euclidean distance) to α, having zero factor risk:

$$\min \; (\alpha - \mathbf{x})'(t\alpha - \mathbf{x})$$

$$\text{s.t. } \mathbf{B}'\mathbf{x} = 0$$

For a given t and ignoring the constraint on the gross market value, the solution is given by

$$\mathbf{x} = (I - \mathbf{B}(\mathbf{B}'\mathbf{B})^{-1}\mathbf{B}')\alpha$$

Note that the formula for $\mathbf{x}$ is the formulas for the residuals η of the linear regression $t\alpha = \mathbf{B}'\beta + \mathbf{x}$. $\mathbf{x}$ is a modified α, in which we have eliminated all collinearity with factor loadings. For more information on this classic problem in optimization and functional analysis and its relationship to regression, see chapters 3 and 4 of [Luenberger, 1969]. We then can scale the vector such that a GMV requirement is satisfied:

$$\mathbf{w} = \frac{\text{GMV}}{\sum_i |x_i|}\mathbf{x}$$

A variant of this problem is the one in which we require the predicted volatility of the portfolio to meet a certain target σ^2, instead of the GMV: $b\mathbf{x}'\Omega_e\mathbf{x} = \sigma^2$; note that $\mathbf{x}'\Omega_r\mathbf{x} = \mathbf{x}'\Omega_e\mathbf{x}$, because the factor risk component of the portfolio is zero.

$$\mathbf{w} = \frac{\sigma}{\sqrt{\mathbf{x}'\Omega_e\mathbf{x}}}\mathbf{x}$$

11.5   Generating Custom Factors

We have a new data source that allows us to create a new "characteristic" for each stock in our coverage. Our objective is to determine whether it has any informative value for our alpha. Let $\mathbf{c}_t \in \mathbb{R}^n$ be the *characteristic vector* at time t; $c_{t,i}$ is the characteristic of asset i available at close of date $t - 1$. We also call this the *custom loading* vector of the assets.

The steps for testing the loadings are:

1. Feature generation;
2. Return estimation;
3. PnL attribution;
4. Evaluation of incremental performance.

Feature Generation. This is the process that takes as input the raw data and outputs a meaningful characteristic vector $\mathbf{c}_t$. In part, feature generation is an art. For example, an observation by Eugene

Fama is that many financial ratios use market cap or similar measures of size to normalize the raw data. If the numerator (raw data) has lower turnover than the denominator (market cap), this characteristic behaves like an inverse of the size factor. In order to make the denominator more stable, a useful practice is to take the equal-weighted average of the denominator over a rolling period (usually 21 days); a similar reasoning applies to normalization by Average Daily Trading Volume (averaging here is usually longer, e.g., 63 days). Some transformations that should be considered at this stage are:

- *Normalization*: by market cap, trading volume, or other firm-specific quantity (e.g., enterprise value, total debt, assets);
- *Interaction*: we can multiply raw characteristics with the loadings of a different factor, or take the asset-wise maximum of the loadings with this factor. A very common application of this transformation is the multiplication of the custom loadings by industry or sector proxies, so that the only non-zero terms are the ones belonging to a sector of interest.
- *Cross-sectional transformations.* These transformations are usually monotonic. Most common transformations are
  - logarithmic transformation: only the order of magnitude of a quantity matters: $y = \log(x)$. The size factor is an example;
  - square-root transformation: $y = \sqrt{x}$. Trading volume terms sometimes use this form;
  - square transformation: $y = x^2$. Nonlinear versions of factors (like nonlinear beta) are based on this transformation;
  - Box-Cox transformation: for some $\lambda > 0$,

$$y = \frac{x^\lambda - 1}{\lambda}$$

   of which the previous three instances are special cases (log transformation as limit case $\lambda \to 0$).
  - ranking: $y = \sum_{i=1}^{N} H(x - x_i)/N$, where N is the number of assets and $H(x) = 0$ if $x < 0$, 1 otherwise. y is uniformly distributed and taking bounded values in $(0, 1)$.
  - arctan transformation: $y = \arctan(x)$. Like ranking, this maps the raw data to a bounded interval $(-1, 1)$.
- *Time-series transformations* are also important. Among these, we highlight three:

- Changes in loadings/trends: $y_t = x_t - x_{t-1}$.
- Changes vs. average levels: $y_t = x_t - n^{-1} \sum_{i=1}^{n} x_{t-i}$.
- Term structure, in which we generalize the change transformation by computing non-overlapping changes in x_t, say, past-day change, past-month change excluding past-day change, and past-year change excluding past month. Momentum is a prominent example.

• *Standardize characteristics.* Let μ_t be the average loading, and σ_t its standard deviation. The standardized loadings are $(c_{t,i} - \mu_t)/\sigma_t$. This is not a strictly necessary step, but it has two benefits. First, standardization helps in interpreting the loadings. Second, if we standardize, the estimated custom factor return can be interpreted as the custom factor return in excess of the market: the factor return is the same whether or not we include an intercept in the regression below. This intercept can be interpreted as the return of a factor, whose loadings are identically equal to one for every asset.

Return Estimation. The returns of the thematic factor are estimated against total returns and residual returns:

$$\mathbf{r}_t = g_t^{tot}\mathbf{c}_t + \eta_t^{tot}$$

$$\epsilon_t = g_t^{res}\mathbf{c}_t + \eta_t^{res}$$

The estimation is performed using weighted least squares, similar to Section 11.1.2. We focus on idiosyncratic return estimation. The estimand g_t^{res} is the custom factor return. We solve the problem

$$\min \ (\epsilon_t - g_t^{res}\mathbf{c}_t)'\mathbf{W}_t(\epsilon_t - g_t^{res}\mathbf{c}_t)$$

$$\text{s.t. } g_t^{res} \in \mathbb{R}$$

The solution in closed form is

$$g_t^{res} = \frac{\mathbf{c}_t'\mathbf{W}_t\epsilon_t}{\mathbf{c}_t'\mathbf{W}_t\mathbf{c}_t}$$

We have a sequence of factors $g_1, \ldots, g_t$, which we can use for risk prediction and performance attribution (briefly described below). Similarly, we have

$$g_t^{tot} = \frac{\mathbf{c}_t'\mathbf{W}_t\mathbf{r}_t}{\mathbf{c}_t'\mathbf{W}_t\mathbf{c}_t}$$

It is possible to reconcile the two regressions resulting in g_t^{res}, g_t^{tot}, in the sense that it is possible to obtain g_t^{res} as the result of the estimation against total returns, $r_t = g_t^{res}\tilde{c}_t + \eta_t^{tot}$, with a special choice of the characteristic vector. The idea is to apply a final transformation, the *orthogonalization* on $\mathbf{c}$, by regressing it by the columns of the matrix $\mathbf{B}_t$ and taking the residuals as loading vector, i.e., the component of $\mathbf{c}_t$ that is not explained by the columns of the matrix $\mathbf{B}_t$. Specifically, we perform two steps (dropping the time subscript for brevity):

1. regress $\mathbf{c} = \mathbf{B}a + \tilde{\mathbf{c}}$ with weight matrix $\mathbf{W}$;
2. regress $\mathbf{r} = \tilde{g}\tilde{\mathbf{c}} + \eta^{tot}$ with weight matrix $\mathbf{W}$.

The output of the first regression is

$$\tilde{\mathbf{c}} = (\mathbf{B} - \mathbf{B}(\mathbf{B}'\mathbf{W}\mathbf{B})^{-1}\mathbf{B}'\mathbf{W})\mathbf{c}$$

Recall that $\epsilon = (\mathbf{B} - \mathbf{B}'\mathbf{W}^2\mathbf{B})^{-1}\mathbf{B}'\mathbf{W})\mathbf{r}$. Therefore

$$\mathbf{c}'\mathbf{W}\epsilon = \mathbf{c}'[\mathbf{W}(\mathbf{B} - \mathbf{B}(\mathbf{B}'\mathbf{W}\mathbf{B})^{-1}\mathbf{B}'\mathbf{W})\mathbf{r}]$$
$$= [\mathbf{c}'(\mathbf{B} - \mathbf{B}(\mathbf{B}'\mathbf{W}\mathbf{B})^{-1}\mathbf{B}'\mathbf{W})]\mathbf{r}$$
$$= \tilde{\mathbf{c}}'\mathbf{W}\mathbf{r}$$
$$\tilde{\mathbf{c}}'\mathbf{W}\tilde{\mathbf{c}} = \mathbf{c}'(\mathbf{B} - \mathbf{B}(\mathbf{B}'\mathbf{W}\mathbf{B})^{-1}\mathbf{B}'\mathbf{W})\mathbf{W}(\mathbf{B} - \mathbf{B}(\mathbf{B}'\mathbf{W}\mathbf{B})^{-1}\mathbf{B}'\mathbf{W})\mathbf{c}$$
$$= \mathbf{c}'\mathbf{W}\mathbf{c}$$

It follows that

$$\tilde{g} = \frac{\tilde{\mathbf{c}}'\mathbf{W}\mathbf{r}}{\tilde{\mathbf{c}}'\mathbf{W}\tilde{\mathbf{c}}} = \frac{\mathbf{c}'\mathbf{W}\epsilon}{\mathbf{c}'\mathbf{W}\mathbf{c}} = g^{res} \tag{11.3}$$

Hence the regression of residual returns is just a modified regression against total returns.

Lastly, we can interpret Equation (11.3) as

$$\tilde{g} = \mathbf{x}'\mathbf{r}$$

where

$$\mathbf{x} = \frac{\mathbf{W}\tilde{\mathbf{c}}}{\tilde{\mathbf{c}}'\mathbf{W}\tilde{\mathbf{c}}}$$

is the portfolio that has the return of the custom factor.

11.5.1   Interpretation and Use

Custom factors can be used both for risk decomposition and performance attribution. We focus on the latter, since this is the main use case. Attribution follows the same procedure in all cases above. First, compute the exposure of the portfolio to the custom factor. If $w_{t,i}$ is the net market value of the portfolio at close of day $t-1$, the exposure at time is $w_t'c_t$, or $w_t'\beta_t$; the attributed PnL is either $w_t'c_t g_t$ (for characteristic custom factors) or $w_t'\beta_t h_t$ (for time-series custom factors). For idiosyncratic return attribution, the interpretation is very similar between the cross-sectional and time-series-based procedures. The PnL is what can be explained in excess of the risk model factor model explanation of PnL. For total return attribution, the explanations of cross-sectional and time-series differ slightly. Cross-sectional PnL attribution provides the strategy's PnL that has not been explained by market return. Time-series PnL attribution also attributes to the custom factor some of the market return to the factor.

11.6   Optimization Formulations

11.6.1   Equal-Sized Portfolio with Constraints on Participation Rate

This subsection describes the liquidity-aware equal-sized portfolio optimization formulation presented in subsection 8.2.1. The sides of the stocks $s_{t,i} = 1/-1$ and the GMV G_t of the portfolio at time t are inputs, derived from the strategy we are analyzing.

Let:

$s_{t,i}$: the sign of stock i on date t, 1/-1 for long/short respectively;

v_i : the average daily trading volume of asset i;

p : the maximum participation rate;

G_t : the target GMV on date t. Alternative parameter: $\tilde{\sigma}_t$ the target idio portfolio idiosyncratic volatility on date t;

σ_f : the maximum factor risk;

$\mathbf{x}_t$: the portfolio vector at time t;

$\mathbf{b}_t$: the vector of factor exposures for portfolio $\mathbf{x}_t$.

$|\mathbf{x}|$: the sum of the absolute values of the elements of $\mathbf{x}$: $\sum_i |x_i|$.

The equal-sized solution problem is a sequence of problems for each period $t = 1, \ldots, T$, as follows:

$$\text{OPT: min } |\mathbf{x}_t - z\mathbf{s}_t| \qquad \qquad (\textit{minimize distance from ideal portfolio})$$

$$\text{s.t. } |[\mathbf{x}_t - \mathbf{x}_{t-1}]_i| \leq pv_i \qquad (\textit{do not exceed participation rate})$$

$$\mathbf{b}_t' \mathbf{\Omega}_{f_t} \mathbf{b}_t \leq \sigma_f^2 \qquad \qquad (\textit{do not exceed max factor risk})$$

$$\mathbf{b}_t = \mathbf{B}_t' \mathbf{x}_t \qquad \qquad (\textit{meet factor exposure identity})$$

$$|\mathbf{x}_t| = G_t \qquad \qquad (\textit{meet GMV requirement})$$

$$z \geq 0 \qquad \qquad (\textit{scale ideal portfolio by z})$$

This is a convex optimization problem that is solvable with commercial solvers. The formulation above targets dynamic GMV, not portfolio variance or idiosyncratic portfolio variance. It is not possible to add a constraint of the form $\sum_i \sigma_i^2 x_{t,i}^2 = \sigma^2$ because the feasible region is non-convex when we add this constraint, resulting in a problem that is difficult to solve and whose solution would be hard to interpret. A workaround is to iterate for different values of the GMV parameter G_t, until the constraint $\sum_i \sigma_i^2 x_{t,i}^2 = \sigma_t^2$ is satisfied.

The procedure is then the following:

Procedure 11.1 alpha testing

---

1. **inputs:** s_t, G_t (or σ_t), $\sigma_f, \mathbf{\Omega}_{f_t}, p$.
2. set $x_0 = 0$.
3. for $t = 1, \ldots, T - 1$, solve OPT using $\mathbf{x}_{t-1}$ as input and obtain $\mathbf{x}_t$ as output.
4. **outputs:** performance metrics (PnL, returns, Sharpe Ratio) on the time series $\mathbf{x}_1' \mathbf{r}_1, \ldots, \mathbf{x}_{T-1}' \mathbf{r}_{T-1}$.

11.7   Tactical Portfolio Optimization

Let:

    $\mathbf{w}$: starting portfolio.

    $\mathbf{x}$: traded portfolio.

$\mathbf{C}$: matrix of custom factor loadings. These could include short interest, hedge fund ownership data, ESG loadings, yield sensitivity.

TC : market impact model.

$$TC(x) = \kappa \sum_i \sigma_i^\beta (|x_i|/v_i)^\gamma$$

where v_i is the average daily trading volume (in dollars), σ_i the volatility, $\beta \simeq 1$, $\gamma \simeq 3/2$ and $\kappa > 0$ a region-calibrated constant.

$\mathbf{l}^b, \mathbf{u}^b$: lower and upper bounds on factor exposures (usually, but not always, $\mathbf{l}^b = -\mathbf{u}^b$).

$\mathbf{l}^c, \mathbf{u}^c$: lower and upper bounds on custom exposures (usually, but not always, $\mathbf{l}^c = -\mathbf{u}^c$).

$\mathbf{d}$: vector of idiosyncratic volatility.

σ_f, σ_t : upper bounds for factor risk and total risk respectively.

g : lower bound on "edge" or on GMV.

E : maximum tracking error between initial and final portfolio.

The optimization problem we solve is:

$$\min\ TC(\mathbf{x})$$

$$\begin{aligned}
\text{s.t. } & \mathbf{v} = \mathbf{w} + \mathbf{x} && (\textit{final portfolio}) \\
& ||\mathbf{x}|| \leq E^2 && (\textit{maximum tracking error}) \\
& \mathbf{w} + \mathbf{x} \geq \mathbf{y} && (\textit{ancillary variable for gmv}) \\
& -(\mathbf{w} + \mathbf{x}) \geq \mathbf{z} && (\textit{ancillary variable for gmv}) \\
& \mathbf{b} = \mathbf{B'v} && (\textit{final exposures}) \\
& \mathbf{c} = \mathbf{C'v} && (\textit{final custom exposures}) \\
& \mathbf{b'\Omega_f b} \leq \sigma_f^2 && (\textit{final factor risk bound}) \\
& \mathbf{l}^b \leq \mathbf{b} \leq \mathbf{u}^b && (\textit{final exposure bounds}) \\
& \mathbf{l}^c \leq \mathbf{c} \leq \mathbf{u}^c && (\textit{final custom exposure bounds}) \\
& \sum_i (y_i + z_i) \geq g && (\textit{minimum GMV}) \\
& \mathbf{y} \geq 0 \\
& \mathbf{z} \geq 0
\end{aligned}$$

11.7.1 Variants

As alternative formulations, allow the user to select as objective function to be one of two:

1. "distance" from starting portfolio, defined as $\mathbf{x}'\mathbf{x}$.
2. "idio tracking error", defined as $\mathbf{x}'\mathbf{\Omega}_\epsilon\mathbf{x}$.

11.8   Hedging Formulations

Let $\mathbf{w} \in \mathbb{R}^p$ be a portfolio with p usually much smaller than n, the universe of investable assets, with factor exposures $\mathbf{b}$. The goal of hedging is to remove from the portfolio the factor return component $\mathbf{b}'\mathbf{f}$.

We consider several alternatives. In these formulations, we will ignore transaction costs, because the focus here is on understanding the essential properties of hedging, and transaction costs can be included in the implementation phase.

Internal Hedging. One option is to hedge the portfolio by trading only the assets in the core portfolio itself; we call this *internal hedging*. Our objective is to change the original portfolio as little as possible. Let $\mathbf{\Omega} \in \mathbb{R}^{p \times p}$ a positive-definite matrix; and let $\tilde{\mathbf{B}} \in \mathbb{R}^{p \times m}$ a matrix that is the subset of rows of $\mathbf{B}$ corresponding to the p assets of $\mathbf{w}$, We solve

$$\text{INTERNAL: min } \mathbf{h}'\mathbf{\Omega}\mathbf{h} \qquad (\textit{minimize size of hedge book})$$

$$\text{s.t. } \tilde{\mathbf{B}}'(\mathbf{w} + \mathbf{h}) = 0 \quad (\textit{no combined factor exposure})$$

When $\mathbf{\Omega}$ is the identity matrix, the objective function is just the square of the euclidean distance between the two vectors; when it is the asset covariance matrix, it is the *tracking error* between the initial and final portfolios, a measure of volatility-adjusted distance. The problem has solution

$$\mathbf{h}^\star = -\mathbf{\Omega}^{-1}\tilde{\mathbf{B}}(\tilde{\mathbf{B}}'\mathbf{\Omega}^{-1}\tilde{\mathbf{B}})^{-1}\tilde{\mathbf{B}}'\mathbf{w} = -\mathbf{\Omega}^{-1}\mathbf{B}(\tilde{\mathbf{B}}'\mathbf{\Omega}^{-1}\tilde{\mathbf{B}})^{-1}\mathbf{b}$$

The resulting combined portfolio $\mathbf{w} + \mathbf{h}$ has zero factor risk but, unless the original portfolio has zero factor exposures, it changes the individual positions of the core portfolio. When $\mathbf{\Omega}$ is the identity matrix, the portfolio contains the entire investment universe (i.e., we allow trading all assets in the universe, including those we don't own), and the portfolio is proportional to the alpha signals, i.e., $\mathbf{w} = \alpha$, the combined portfolio is

$$\mathbf{w} + \mathbf{h}^\star = (I - \mathbf{B}(\mathbf{B}'\mathbf{B})^{-1}\mathbf{B}')\alpha$$

This is the first step in Procedure 6.3; in other words, $\mathbf{x}^\star$ is the vector of residuals of a regression of $\mathbf{w}$ on the columns of $\mathbf{B}$.

External Hedging. The hedging problem is one in which we want to minimize risk by trading factor-mimicking portfolios while constraining the size of the hedge book. Since the factor-mimicking portfolios[2] (FMPs) are the columns of $\mathbf{V}$, the hedge book takes the form $\mathbf{h} = \mathbf{Vx}$; x_i is the number of units of the "factor i synthetic asset that we are buying for hedging purposes". A constraint on $\mathbf{h}$ takes the form $\mathbf{h}'\mathbf{Dh} \leq L$, where $\mathbf{D}$ is a positive-definite matrix that induces a distance in $\mathbb{R}^n$. If $\mathbf{D} = \mathbf{\Omega}_r$, then we are imposing a requirement on the volatility of the hedging portfolio; if $\mathbf{D} = I$, then we are imposing a constraint on the deviation of the final portfolio $\mathbf{w} + \mathbf{h}$ from the initial one, $\mathbf{w}$. This can be interpreted as a requirement that the original sizing positions of the portfolio be not excessively altered by the hedge book.

EXTERNAL: min $(\mathbf{w} + \mathbf{h})'\mathbf{\Omega}_r(\mathbf{w} + \mathbf{h})$ (*minimize total risk*)

s.t. $\mathbf{h}'\mathbf{Dh} \leq L$ (*constraint on max hedge size or tracking error*)

$\mathbf{h} = \mathbf{Vx}$ (*linking hedging exposures to hedge portfolio*)

$\mathbf{x} \in \mathbb{R}^m$

$\mathbf{h} \in \mathbb{R}^n$

It is important to minimize *total risk*, and not just factor risk. Factor-mimicking portfolios contain idiosyncratic risk, and this risk should not be ignored. In applications, there will be a penalty for transaction costs, and additional linear constraints, e.g., of the form $|b_i + x_i| \leq E_i$ on maximum individual factor exposures of the combined book. We ignore these constraints to illustrate the properties of the optimal hedge in an ideal environment of frictionless market. We "price out" the inequality constraint as a penalty in the objective

---

[2] Defined in Section 11.1.2.

function and solve

$$\min \ (\mathbf{w} + \mathbf{Vx})' \mathbf{\Omega}_r (\mathbf{w} + \mathbf{Vx}) + \lambda \mathbf{x}' \mathbf{V}' \mathbf{D} \mathbf{Vx} \qquad (11.4)$$

s.t. $\mathbf{x} \in \mathbb{R}^m$

where $\lambda > 0$ is a penalty constant.

The first-order condition for the problem is

$$\mathbf{V}'(\mathbf{B}\mathbf{\Omega}_f \mathbf{B}' + \mathbf{\Omega}_e)(\mathbf{w} + \mathbf{Vx}) + \lambda \mathbf{V}' \mathbf{D} \mathbf{Vx} = 0$$

which is solved for

$$\mathbf{x}^\star = -[\mathbf{\Omega}_f + (\mathbf{B}'\mathbf{\Omega}_e^{-1}\mathbf{B})^{-1} + \lambda \mathbf{V}'\mathbf{D}\mathbf{V}]^{-1}(\mathbf{\Omega}_f \mathbf{b} + \mathbf{V}'\mathbf{\Omega}_e \mathbf{w}) \qquad (11.5)$$

This solution seems involved, but it covers a lot of ground. Let us consider a few cases.

- When the factor portfolios are "pure" (i.e., they have no idiosyncratic risk), and the tracking error constraint is loose (i.e., for large values of L), then we are in the ideal regime. As per as Eq. (11.1), the covariance matrix of idiosyncratic returns for the factor-mimicking portfolios is $(\mathbf{B}'\mathbf{\Omega}_e^{-1}\mathbf{B})^{-1}$, and it is negligible compared to $\mathbf{\Omega}_f$, we can ignore it in Eq. (11.5). When L is large, λ is small, so we can ignore the term $\lambda \mathbf{V}'\mathbf{D}\mathbf{V}$. Finally $\mathbf{V}^{-1}\mathbf{\Omega}_e\mathbf{w}$ is the vector of covariances of the factor-mimicking portfolios with the core portfolio. If the factor portfolio has negligible idio vol, then this term can also be ignored. After all of these simplifications, the optimal hedge is $\mathbf{x}^\star = -\mathbf{b}$. This is the "naïve" hedge.
- Let us keep the assumption of low idio covariance between factor-mimicking portfolios and the core portfolio; this is a realistic assumption. But now let us admit the case that the factors are impure and that the tracking error constraint is binding. This use case is the most likely to occur in practice. After factoring out $\mathbf{\Omega}_f$, the optimal solution becomes

$$\mathbf{x}^\star = -[\mathbf{\Omega}_f + (\mathbf{B}'\mathbf{\Omega}_e^{-1}\mathbf{B})^{-1} + \lambda \mathbf{V}'\mathbf{D}\mathbf{V}]^{-1}\mathbf{\Omega}_f \mathbf{b} \qquad (11.6)$$

$$\simeq [-I + \mathbf{\Omega}_f^{-1}((\mathbf{B}'\mathbf{\Omega}_e^{-1}\mathbf{B})^{-1} + \lambda \mathbf{V}'\mathbf{D}\mathbf{V})]\mathbf{b}$$

Where the approximate inequality is a first-order expansion of the Neumann series. We deviate from "naïve" hedging. To a first approximation, we always hedge *less* than in the "naïve" hedge in the following sense: the optimal hedge is $\mathbf{x}^\star = (-I + \mathbf{\Omega}_f^{-1}\mathbf{H})\mathbf{b}$, where $\mathbf{H} =$

$(\mathbf{B}'\boldsymbol{\Omega}_{\varepsilon}^{-1}\mathbf{B})^{-1} + \lambda\mathbf{V}'\mathbf{D}\mathbf{V}$ is a positive definite matrix that has norm smaller than one. The factor variance of the "naïve" hedge is $\mathbf{b}'\boldsymbol{\Omega}_f\mathbf{b}$ and of the optimal hedge is $(\mathbf{x}^\star)'\boldsymbol{\Omega}_f\mathbf{x}^\star$. We show that $(\mathbf{x}^\star)'\boldsymbol{\Omega}_f\mathbf{x}^\star < \mathbf{b}'\boldsymbol{\Omega}_f\mathbf{b}$; this follows from

$$(\mathbf{x}^\star)'\boldsymbol{\Omega}_f\mathbf{x}^\star = \mathbf{b}'\boldsymbol{\Omega}_f\mathbf{b} - 2\mathbf{b}'\mathbf{H}'\mathbf{b} + (\textit{second-order term}) < \mathbf{b}'\boldsymbol{\Omega}_f\mathbf{b}$$

- Let us stay in the regime of pure factor-mimicking portfolios. When L is very low, meaning that the hedge book is forced to remain small, the penalization constant λ is high. In this limit we have

$$\mathbf{x}^\star = -\frac{1}{\lambda}(\mathbf{V}'\mathbf{D}\mathbf{V})^{-1}\boldsymbol{\Omega}_f\mathbf{b} \qquad (11.7)$$

  The hedge is smaller as the tracking error constraint becomes more binding.

This analysis serves two purposes. First, Equations (11.5, 11.6, 11.7) are useful as first numerical approximations to hedge solutions. It is easy to maintain closed-form solutions when we add quadratic market impacts and linear constraints. Second, it shows that the optimal hedge is not the opposite of the exposures, as is commonly believed. Even when we do not have size constraints on the hedge book ($L \gg 0$ or $\lambda = 0$), we may have a factor-mimicking portfolio with a high percentage idio volatility; in that case we don't want to hedge fully. Additionally, when we have constraints on the hedge book size, then obviously we will hedge less than the core portfolio factor exposures, and Eq. (11.5) tells us how.

A revised version of the original problem, with transaction costs and linear constraints is below.

EXTERNAL$'$: min $(\mathbf{w} + \mathbf{h})'\boldsymbol{\Omega}_r(\mathbf{w} + \mathbf{h})$ (*minimize total risk*)

         s.t. $\mathbf{h}'\mathbf{D}\mathbf{h} \leq L$ (*constraint on max hedge size or tracking error*)

             $\mathbf{h} = \mathbf{V}\mathbf{x} + \mathbf{v}$ (*linking hedging exposures to hedge portfolio*)

             $TCOST(\mathbf{h} - \mathbf{h}_0) \leq C$ (*impact from trading* $\mathbf{h} - \mathbf{h}_0$)

             $\mathbf{v}'\mathbf{v} \leq M$ (*constraint on max deviation or tracking error from FMPs*)

             $A'(\mathbf{w} + \mathbf{h}) \leq \mathbf{c}$ (*additional linear constraints*)

             $\mathbf{x} \in \mathbb{R}^m$

             $\mathbf{v} \in \mathbb{R}^n$

             $\mathbf{h} \in \mathbb{R}^n$

There are equivalent formulations, which I omit for the sake of brevity, in which we minimize market impact subject to an upper bound on total risk. The current formulation relies on three inputs, set by the decision maker:

C : the maximum transaction cost;

L : the maximum tracking error (or 2-norm) of the hedge book;

M : the maximum deviation, measured as volatility or 2-norm, from a pure FMP-based hedge.

If L and C are large enough to be non-binding, and if $M = 0$, then the optimal hedging is the same as a pure FMP-based hedge. In practice, it is useful to explore the performance of the hedged portfolio varying all three parameters.

11.9   Optimal Event Trading

Consider a single asset with price $P(t)$. We assume that the asset is infinitely divisible (we can buy arbitrarily small amounts of it) and that it can be shorted at zero cost in arbitrary amounts. The investor holds $x(t)$ dollars' worth of the asset. The trading volume is varying over time. We assume it is constant: "time" in this section refers to "volume time": the total traded volume in a time interval is proportional to the interval length.[3] Therefore, physical time intervals in which volume is high correspond to longer intervals in volume time. The return process in the interval $[0, T]$ is

$$dP(t) = P(t)[\alpha(t)dt + \sigma\,dB(t)]$$

$$P(0) = 1$$

---

[3] Volume time can be computed based on realized or forecasted trading volume $v(t)$. Let $V(t) = \int_0^t v(s)ds$, and define $\tau = V(t)$. The volume traded in the interval $[\tau, \tau + \delta]$ is constant. It is equal to the volume traded in the interval $[V^{-1}(\tau), V^{-1}(\tau) + (V^{-1})'(\tau)\delta]$, which is

$$V'(V^{-1}(\tau)) \times [(V^{-1})'(\tau)\delta] = V'(V^{-1}(\tau)) \times \left[\frac{\delta}{V'(V^{-1}(\tau))}\right] = \delta$$

We make two assumptions:

1. *Alpha curve*: The function $\alpha(t)$ is known in $[0, T]$.
2. *Quadratic transaction costs*: The transaction costs associated to trading a dollar amount v of the stock are proportional to v^2. We write

$$TC(v) = \frac{\kappa^2}{2}v^2 \qquad (11.8)$$

The general problem is

$$\max_x \int_0^T \left(\alpha(t)x(t) - \frac{\kappa^2}{2}\dot{x}^2(t) - \frac{\rho\sigma^2}{2}x^2(t) \right) dt$$

$$\text{s.t. } x(0) = 0$$

$$x(T) = 0$$

where

- αx is the expected return;
- $(\kappa^2/2)\dot{x}^2$ is the transaction cost;
- $(\rho\sigma^2/2)x^2$ is the risk aversion term.

Before producing examples and analytical processes, we discuss the model assumptions and their limits. We assume that the function α is known by the investor. This seems a reasonable assumption, since the investor does have a view of the stock returns over the horizon. However, we do not model two important components of the investor's information. First, the investor may have different conviction for the stock alpha at a given time. If the stock has an earning announcement, then the α view on that date will be stronger than for preceding days. The second assumption we make is that no new information is acquired during the investment and α is not updated based on the information. However, new information arrives all the time, both in the form of company-specific news and market participant information. The stock may experience a run-up, and this run-up may be interpreted as other investors acting on the same information contained in α. In this event, we would either need to update α, or model the investment problem in an altogether different way. The assumption of quadratic transaction costs is also an idealization. Transaction cost models usually include a linear term and a polynomial one, which has an exponent between 2/3 and 2. The assumption is not unrealistic because the exponent estimated from empirical data is closer to 2, and the linear term is much smaller than the polynomial one. We also make the assumption that κ is constant. This seems acceptable, so long as market conditions do not change; typical horizons for this problem are a month or less.

Optimal Policy. Write the objective function as

$$\int_0^T L(t, x, \dot{x})dt, \text{ where } L(t, x, \dot{x}) = \alpha x - \frac{\kappa^2}{2}\dot{x}^2 - \frac{\rho^2\sigma^2}{2}x^2$$

The Euler-Lagrange equation is

$$\partial_x L - \frac{d}{dt}\partial_{\dot{x}}L = 0, \text{ i.e., } \kappa^2\ddot{x} = -\alpha + \rho^2\sigma^2 x$$

This is a non-homogeneous linear ordinary differential equation. Let us define

$$a = \alpha/\kappa^2$$

$$b = \rho\sigma/\kappa$$

$$F(t) = \int_0^t \frac{a(\zeta)e^{b\zeta}}{2b}d\zeta$$

$$G(t) = \int_0^t \frac{a(\zeta)e^{-b\zeta}}{2b}d\zeta$$

The solution is given by

$$x(t) = e^{-bt}(F(t) + c) - e^{bt}(G(t) + c)$$

$$c = \frac{e^{-bT}F(T) - e^{bT}G(T)}{e^{bT} - e^{-bT}}$$

The trading rate $\dot{x}$ is more instructive, and is equal to

$$\dot{x}(t) = e^{-bt}[\dot{F}(t) - bF(t) - bc] - e^{bt}[\dot{G}(t) + bG(t) + bc]$$

The formulas hold for any forecasted time-varying alpha. We are interested in the special case of *event-based return*:

$$\alpha(t) = \alpha_0\delta(t - t_0)$$

where $\delta(\cdot)$ is Dirac's delta.[4] There is a single event, e.g., an earning announcement. In this case

$$F(t) = \frac{\alpha_0 e^{bt_0}}{2\sigma\rho\kappa}\theta(t - t_0) = K_F\theta(t - t_0)$$

$$G(t) = \frac{\alpha_0 e^{-bt_0}}{2\sigma\rho\kappa}\theta(t - t_0) = K_G\theta(t - t_0)$$

$$c = \frac{e^{-bT}K_F - e^{bT}K_G}{e^{bT} - e^{-bT}}$$

$$\dot{x}(t) = e^{-bt}\left(\frac{\alpha_0 e^{bt_0}}{2\sigma\rho\kappa}\delta(t - t_0) - bF - bc\right) -$$

$$e^{bt}\left(\alpha_0\frac{e^{-bt_0}}{2\sigma\rho\kappa}\delta(t - t_0) + bG + bc\right)$$

$$= -be^{-bt}(F + c) - be^{bt}(G + c)$$

$$= \begin{cases} -bc(e^{-bt} + e^{bt}) & \text{if } t \le t_0 \\ -be^{-bt}(K_F + c) - be^{bt}(K_G + c) & \text{if } t > t_0 \end{cases}$$

Note that $K_G = e^{-2bt_0}K_F$ and $c < 0$. As an example, assume that $\alpha_0 > 0$. The trading policy is to trade on the side of α_0 up to the event. The trade is not linear. After t_0, trading is in the opposite direction:

$$K_G = e^{-2bt_0}K_F$$

$$K_F + c \ge K_G + c$$

$$= K_G(e^{bT} - e^{-bT}) - (e^{-bT}K_F - e^{bT}K_G)$$

$$= K_G e^{bT}[1 - e^{-2b(T-t_0)}]$$

$$\ge 0$$

so that both terms in the formula for $t \ge t_0$ are negative.

Since there is no natural liquidation horizon T, it is useful to consider for practical applications the case $T \to \infty$.

---

[4] Dirac's delta $\delta(\cdot)$ is a generalized function equal to 0 for $x \ne 0$ and such that $\int_{-\infty}^{\infty} \delta(x)dx = 1$. An associated function is Heavyside's function $\theta(\cdot)$, which is equal to 0 for $x < 0$ and to 1 for $x \ge 0$.

Optimal Policy with Long-Horizon Liquidation. In this limit we have $c \to -K_G$, and

$$x(t) = e^{-bt}(F(t) - K_G) - e^{bt}(G(t) - K_G)$$

$$= \begin{cases} \frac{\alpha_0}{b\kappa^2} e^{-bt_0} \sinh(bt) & \text{if } t \leq t_0 \\\\ \frac{\alpha_0}{b\kappa^2} \sinh(bt_0)e^{-bt} & \text{if } t > t_0 \end{cases}$$

The optimal policy is to build the position and then to liquidate it, at a fast rate right after the event, and then more and more slowly. The optimal position at event date t_0 is

$$x(t_0) = \frac{\alpha_0}{2b\kappa^2}(1 - e^{-2bt_0})$$

The optimal trading rate is

$$\dot{x}(t) = \begin{cases} \frac{\alpha_0 e^{-bt_0}}{\kappa^2} \cosh(bt) & \text{if } t \leq t_0 \\\\ -\frac{\alpha_0}{\kappa^2} \sinh(bt_0)e^{-bt} & \text{if } t > t_0 \end{cases}$$

Just prior to the event and after the event the trading rate is identical in size but opposite in direction:

$$\text{trading rate just before } t = t_0 : \frac{\alpha_0}{2\kappa^2}(1 + e^{-2bt_0})$$

$$\text{trading rate just after } t = t_0 : -\frac{\alpha_0}{2\kappa^2}(1 + e^{-2bt_0})$$

Optimal Policy with Long-Horizon Liquidation and Risk-Neutral Investor. In the limit $\rho \to 0$, we have

$$x(t) \simeq \begin{cases} \frac{\alpha_0}{\kappa^2} t & \text{if } t \leq t_0 \\\\ \frac{\alpha_0 t_0}{\kappa^2}(1 - t) & \text{if } t > t_0 \end{cases} \tag{11.9}$$

References

R. Alquist, R. Israel, and T. J. Moskowitz. Fact, fiction, and the size effect. *The Journal of Portfolio Management*, 45(1):3–30, 2018.

L. Angelini, M. Iqbal, and F. Jivraj. Systematic 13f hedge fund alpha. *Barclays QIS Insights*, 2019.

C. S. Asness, T. J. Moskowitz, and L. H. Pedersen. Value and momentum everywhere. *Journal of Finance*, 58(3):929–985, 2013.

C. R. Bacon. *Practical Portfolio Performance Measurement and Attribution*. Wiley, 2005.

R. Banz. The relationship between return and market value of common stock. *Journal of Financial Economics*, 9(1):3–18, 1981.

P. L. Bernstein. *Against the Gods: The Remarkable Story of Risk*. Wiley, 1996.

A. Beveratos, J.-P. Bouchaud, S. Ciliberti, L. Laloux, Y. Lempérière, M. Potters, and G. Simon. Deconstructing the low-vol anomaly. *Journal of Portfolio Management*, 44(1):91–103, 2014.

A. J. Black, B. Mao, and D. G. McMillan. The value premium and economic activity: Long-run evidence from the United States. *Journal of Asset Management*, 10(5):305–317, 2009.

F. Black, M. C. Jensen, and M. Scholes. The capital asset pricing model: Some empirical tests. In M. C. Jensen, editor, *Studies in the Theory of Capital Markets*, pages 79–121. Praeger Publishing Co, 1972.

D. Blitz, E. Falkenstein, and P. van Vliet. Explanations for the volatility effect: An overview based on the CAPM assumptions. *Journal of Portfolio Management*, 40(3):61–76, 2014.

J. B. Buckheit and D. L. Donoho. Wavelab and reproducible statistics. In A. Antoniadis and G. Oppenheim, editors, *Wavelets and Statistics*, pages 55–81. Springer, 1995.

H. Buehler, L. Gonon, J. Teichmann, B. Wood, B. Mohan, and J. Kochems. Deep hedging: Hedging derivatives under generic market frictions using reinforcement learning. *Swiss Finance Institute Research Paper No. 19-80*, 2019.

F. Chabi-Yo, S. Ruenzi, and F. Weigert. Crash sensitivity and the cross section of expected stock returns. *Journal of Financial and Quantitative Analysis*, 53 (3):1059–1100, 2018.

N. Chen and F. Zhang. Risk and return of value stocks. *Journal of Business*, 71(4):501–535, 1988.

Y. Choueifaty and Y. Coignard. Toward maximum diversification. *Journal of Portfolio Management*, 35(1):40–51, 2008.

J. H. Cochrane. New facts in finance. *Economic Perspectives*, 23(3):36–58, 1999.

R. B. Cohen, C. Polk, and B. Silli. Best ideas. *Unpublished*, 2010.

G. Connor and R. A. Korajczyk. Factor models of asset returns. In R. Cont, editor, *Encyclopedia of Quantitative Finance*. Wiley, 2010.

G. Connor, L. R. Goldberg, and R. A. Korajczyk. *Portfolio risk analysis*. Princeton University Press, 2010.

R. Cont. Empirical properties of asset returns: Stylized facts and statistical issues. *Quantitative Finance*, 1:223–236, 2001.

A. Cowles, 3rd and H. E. Jones. Some a posteriori probabilities in stock market action. *Econometrica*, 5(3):280, 294 1937.

Z. Da, U. G. Gurun, and M. Warachka. Frog in the pan: Continuous information and momentum. *Review of Financial Studies*, 27(7):2171–2218, 2014.

K. Daniel and T. J. Moskowitz. Momentum crashes. *Journal of Financial Economics*, 122(2):221–247, 2016.

J. B. Delong, A. Shleifer, L. H. Summers, and R. J. Waldmann. Positive feedback investment strategies and destabilizing rational speculation. *Journal of Finance*, 45(2):379–395, 1990.

V. DeMiguel, L. Garlappi, and R. Uppal. Optimal versus naive diversification: How inefficient is the 1/n portfolio strategy? *Review of Financial Studies*, 22 (5):1915–1953, 2009.

A. Denev and S. Amin. *The Book of Alternative Data*. Wiley, 2020.

K. Diether, C. Malloy, and A. Scherbina. Differences of opinion and the cross section of stock returns. *Journal of Finance*, 57(5):2113–2141, 2002.

K. B. Diether, K.-H. Lee, and I. M. Werner. Short-sale strategies and return predictability. *The Review of Financial Studies*, 22(2):575–607, 2009.

E. W. Dijkstra. On the role of scientific thought. In *Selected Writings on Computing: A personal Perspective*, pages 60–66. Springer, 1982.

G. Epstein. Short can be sweet. *Barron's*, Oct 2, 1995.

F. J. Fabozzi. *Short Selling. Strategies, Risks and Rewards*, chapter Mechanics of the Equity Lending Market. Wiley, 2004.

F. J. Fabozzi, P. N. Kolm, D. A. Pachamanova, and S. M. Focardi. *Robust Portfolio Optimization and Management*. Wiley, 2007.

E. F. Fama and K. R. French. The cross-section of expected stock returns. *Journal of Finance*, 47(2):427–465, 1993.

E. F. Fama and K. R. French. Dissecting anomalies with a five-factor model. *The Review of Financial Studies*, 29(1):69–103, 2016.

E. F. Fama and J. D. MacBeth. Risk, return, and equilibrium: Empirical tests. *Journal of Political Economy*, 81(3):607–636, 1973.

G. M. Frankfurter, H. E. Phillips, and J. P. Seagle. Portfolio selection: The effects of uncertain means, variances and covariances. *Journal of Financial and Quantitative Analysis*, 6(5):1251–1262, 1971.

A. Frazzini and L. H. Pedersen. Betting against beta. *Journal of Financial Economics*, 111(1):1–25, 2014.

X. Gabaix. Power laws in economics and finance. *Annual Review of Economics*, 1:255–93, 2009.

C. Geczy and M. Samonov. Two centuries of price return momentum. *Financial Analysts Journal*, 72(5):32–56, 2016.

A. Goyal and N. Jegadeesh. Cross-sectional and time-series tests of return predictability: What is the difference? *The Review of Financial Studies*, 31 (5):1784–1824, 2018.

J. M. Griffin and M. L. Lemmon. Book-to-market equity, distress risk, and stock returns. *Journal of Finance*, 57(5):2317–2337, 2002.

R. C. Grinold and R. N. Kahn. *Active Portfolio Management*. McGraw-Hill Education, 2nd edition, 1999.

S. J. Grossman and Z. Zhou. Optimal investment strategies for controlling drawdowns. *Mathematical Finance*, 3(3):241–276, 1993.

P. R. Hansen and A. Lunde. A forecast comparison of volatility models: does anything beat a $garch(1, 1)$. *Journal of Applied Econometrics*, 20(7):873–889, 2005.

C. R. Harvey and Y. Liu. Lucky factors. *preprint*, 2015a.

C. R. Harvey and Y. Liu. Backtesting. *Journal of Portfolio Management*, 42 (1):13–28, 2015b.

C. R. Harvey, Y. Liu, and H. Zhu. … and the cross-section of expected returns. *The Review of Financial Studies*, 29(1):5–61, 2016.

C. R. Harvey, E. Hoyle, R. Korgaonar, S. Rattray, M. Sargaison, and O. Van Hemert. The impact of volatility targeting. *Journal of Portfolio Management*, 45(1):14–33, 2018.

N. Jegadeesh and S. Titman. Returns to buying winners and selling losers: implications for stock market efficiency. *Journal of Finance*, 48(1):65–91, 1993.

N. Jegadeesh and S. Titman. Momentum. *Annual Review of Financial Economics*, 3(1):493–509, 2011.

J. D. Jobson and B. Korkie. Estimation for markowitz efficient portfolios. *Journal of the American Statistical Association*, 75(371):544–554, 1980.

E. Jurczenco, editor. *Risk-based and factor investing*. Elsevier, 2015.

M. Kolanovic and R. T. Krishnamachari. Big data and ai strategies: Machine learning and alternative data approach to investing. Technical report, J. P. Morgan, 2017.

P. N. Kolm, R. Tütüncü, and F. J. Fabozzi. 60 years of portfolio optimization: Practical challenges and current trends. *European Journal of Operational Research*, 234:356–371, 2014.

J. Lakonishok, A. Shleifer, and R. W. Vishny. Contrarian investment, extrapolation, and risk. *Journal of Finance*, 49(5):1541–1578, 1994.

O. Ledoit and M. Wolf. Honey, i shrunk the sample covariance matrix: Problems in mean-variance optimization. *Journal of Portfolio Management*, 30:110–119, 2003.

E. Lefèvre. *Reminiscences of a Stock Operator*. George H. Doran Company, 1923.

F. C. Leone, L. S. Nelson, and R. B. Nottingham. The folded normal distribution. *Technometrics*, 3(4):543–550, 1961.

R. Litterman, editor. *Modern Investment Management: An Equilibrium Approach*. Wiley, 2003.

A. W. Lo. The statistics of sharpe ratios. *Financial Analysts Journal*, 58(4): 36–52, 2002.

M. M. López de Prado. *Machine Learning for Asset Managers*. Cambridge University Press, 2020.

T. Loughran and B. McDonald. Textual analysis in accounting and finance: A survey. *Journal of Accounting Research*, 54(4):1187–1230, 2016.

D. G. Luenberger. *Optimization by Vector Space Methods*. Wiley, 1969.

H. M. Markowitz. *Portfolio Selection: Efficient Diversification of Investments*. Basil Blackwell, 2nd edition, 1959.

P. G. Martin and B. B. McCann. *The Investor's Guide to Fidelity Funds*. Wiley, 1989.

A. J. McNeil, R. Frey, and P. Embrechts. *Quantitative Risk Management*. Princeton University Press, 2005.

R. C. Merton. On the pricing of corporate debt: The risk structure of interest rates. *Journal of Finance*, 29(2):449–470, 1974.

A. Moreira and T. Muir. Volatility-managed portfolios. *Journal of Finance*, 72 (4):1611–1644, 2017.

A. Moreira and T. Muir. Should long-term investors time volatility? *Journal of Financial Economics*, 131(3):507–529, 2019.

R. Novy-Marx. Is momentum really momentum? *Journal of Financial Economics*, 103:429–453, 2012.

R. Novy-Marx. Understanding defensive equity. *Working Paper*, 2016.

G. Orwell. Politics and the english language. In S. Orwell and I. Angos, editors, *The Collected Essays, Journalism and Letters of George Orwell*, volume 4, pages 127–140. Harcourt, Brace, Javanovich, 1946.

P. M. Pardalos and S. A. Vavasis. Quadratic programming with one negative eigenvalue is np-hard. *Journal of Global Optimization*, 1(1):15–22, 1991.

L. Petkova. Do the Fama–French factors proxy for innovations in predictive variables? *Journal of Finance*, 61(2):581–612, 2006.

R. Roll. A critique of the asset pricing theory's tests part i: On past and potential testability of the theory. *Journal of Financial Economics*, 4(2): 129–176, 1977.

J. P. Romano and M. Wolf. Stepwise multiple testing as formalized data snooping. *Econometrica*, 73(4):1237–1282, 2005.

B. Rosenberg and V. Marathe. Common factors in security returns: Microeconomic determinants and macroeconomic correlates. In *Working paper series: Graduate School of Business Administration, Research Program in Finance*, 1976. URL https://books.google.com/books?id=qcxttwAACAAJ.

S. Ruenzi and F. Weigert. Momentum and crash sensitivity. *Economic Letters*, 165:77–81, 2018.

SEC. Form 13f: Information required of institutional investment managers pursuant to section 13(f) of the securities exchange act of 1934 and rules thereunder, 1934. URL https://www.sec.gov/pdf/form13f.pdf.

P. Seibel. *Coders at Work: Reflections on the Art of Programming*. Apress, 2009.

R. A. Stubbs and P. Vance. Computing return estimation error matrices for robust optimization. Technical Report 1, Axioma Research Paper, 2005.

M. Goedhart T. Koller and D. Wessels. *Valuation: Measuring and Managing the Value of Companies*. Wiley, 6th edition, 2015.

H. White. A reality check for data snooping. *Econometrica*, 68(5):1097–1126, 2000.

P. Xidonas, R. Steuer, and C. Hassapis. Robust portfolio optimization: a categorized bibliographic review. *Annals of Operations Research*, 292: 533–552, 2020.

Index

$3, 5, 11, 21, 43, 85$

$+2 \quad +6 \quad +10 \quad +22 \quad +42$

$3, 10, 29, 84, 247$

$+7 \quad +19 \quad +55 \quad +163 \quad +3211$
$\quad +12 \quad +36 \quad +108 \quad +12 \cdot 27$

$\times 3 +1 \quad \times 3 -1 \quad \times 3$

$1 \quad -2 \quad 5 \quad 4 \quad 9 \quad -6 \quad 13$

$-3 \quad +7 \quad -1 \quad +5 \quad -15 \quad +19$
$\quad +10 \quad -8 \quad +6 \quad -20 \quad +34$

$5 \quad 24 \quad 8 \quad 48 \quad 15$

$+19 \quad -14 \quad +41 \quad -23$

7^4

$\frac{1}{8} \cdot \frac{1}{2} \frac{1}{2} \left(\frac{5}{8} \right)$

$\frac{1}{7} \cdot \frac{1}{7} \cdot \frac{6}{7} \cdot \frac{6}{7} \times$

$\frac{1}{16} \cdot \frac{1}{2} \left(\frac{5}{4} \right)$

$\binom{4}{2}$

$\frac{1}{32}$

$\frac{1}{32} + \frac{5}{32} + \frac{10}{32}$

$$\frac{1}{5}\cdot\frac{1}{5}\cdot\frac{1}{5}\cdot\frac{1}{5}\cdot\frac{4}{5}\cdot\frac{4}{5}\cdot\frac{4}{5}\cdot\binom{7}{4} \qquad \frac{7\cdot6\cdot5}{3\cdot2}$$

$$\frac{64\cdot35}{78125}$$

$$\frac{64\cdot7}{15625} \qquad \frac{3\cdot6}{29}$$

$$\left(\frac{1}{2^6}\right)\cdot4 + \frac{1}{2^7}\cdot2 + \frac{1}{2^5}$$

$$\frac{7}{2^8}$$

$$\frac{4\cdot3+2+1}{2^5}$$

$$\frac{6}{32}$$